The Mistress from Chandernagore

The Mistress from Chandernagore

A. B. de M. Hunter

Cover: Madame Grand by Elisabeth Vigée Le Brun 1783 (www.metmuseum.org)

Matador
Unit E2 Airfield Business Park,
Harrison Road, Market Harborough,
Leicestershire. LE16 7WB
Tel: 0116 279 2299
Email: books@troubador.co.uk
Web: www.troubador.co.uk/matador
Twitter: @matadorbooks

ISBN 978 1803130 491

British Library Cataloguing in Publication Data.
A catalogue record for this book is available from the British Library.

Printed and bound in Great Britain by 4edge Limited
Typeset in 11pt Adobe Jenson Pro by Troubador Publishing Ltd, Leicester, UK

Matador is an imprint of Troubador Publishing Ltd

L'amour est l'histoire de la vie des femmes;
c'est un épisode dans celle des hommes.

Mme de Staël 1796

Prologue

10 July 1777

'I, George Francois, take thee, Catherine-Noël, to be my wedded wife, to have and to hold from this day forward, for better, for worse, for richer, for poorer, in sickness and in health, to love and to cherish, till death us do part.' George smiled at his young bride as he followed the Reverend Johnson's prompts, aware he had already made the same vow to her in French only a few hou͏ ͏ ͏ at her church in Chandernagore. But this was a pro͏ ͏ ͏ Hooghly House, which ͏ ͏ English colleag͏ ͏ was stunningl͏ ͏ unmarred by ͏ to her relative͏ wore his Chev͏ the French co͏ being able to co͏ parents. Old M͏ marry his daugh͏

India Company; for relations between the two companies were amicable enough here in Bengal. Indeed, the friendship of the two governors, M. Chevalier and Mr Hastings, ensured plenty of mutually lavish hospitality and gay celebration of whichever country's festival fell due. And there had been no doubt who had been the 'belle of the ball'. Though barely a teenager, Catherine was by far the prettiest of the young ladies at Chandernagore, already taller than most, with luxuriant blond hair and a body that looked and moved like a nymph. Yes, indeed, he had secured a real jewel of a wife and knew his friends envied him his good fortune.

At this moment Catherine was completing her recital of the unfamiliar English words: '... according to God's holy ordinance, and thereto I plight thee my troth.' She too was reminded how she had already made her vows that morning: she was already Mrs George Grand, wife of a well-established member of this Calcutta society. Catherine was well pleased with her new husband. Mr Hastings had promoted him on their engagement and, George had told her, it meant he could more than adequately provide for her. There were not many Company writers who could achieve what he had done before his thirtieth year. And he was good company. She had enjoyed being wooed by him in his strange French, supplemented with Bengali phrases as familiar to her as they clearly were to him. Glancing at his friends behind him, she was reminded that she was joining an English community and she had better improve her English if she was to take her proper place in it.

Catherine's father shifted uneasily on his chair. He had felt proud to take Catherine up the aisle of their church in Chandernagore earlier that day, basking in the good wishes of friends and colleagues, French and Bengali alike. Here it was different: the English service did not bother him, as it was as vaguely meaningful to him as his Latin mass. But it was not even being held in a church. They had passed the splendid new houses and busy warehouses that lined the river front, but behind, the ruins of St John's church remained untouched since first destroyed by Siraj ud-Daulah twenty years previously. It spoke volumes for the priorities of the English East India Company. Mind you, the Company was well represented here for the wedding. He noticed Mr Hastings had come to support his protégée, and doubtless was making mental notes for his own wedding next month. There were scarlet uniforms of the Company's military among the more sober hues of the traders and the bright colours of the ladies. Certainly, Catherine was joining a prosperous band of expatriates here in Calcutta, and there was no doubting the love George had for Catherine. Monsieur Worlée smiled as he wondered whether George really knew what he was taking on with her. He knew that behind that sweet expression and those golden tresses there was a fertile mind that had challenged him – and her mother – many a time. She had outshone her brother and sisters and matured fast in the vibrant confines of Chandernagore port. He was sure she was as ready to be married at fourteen as her mother had been at sixteen. Now, with the last of his children married, he could turn his attention to retiring and returning to France, sufficiently well off now to restore the Worlée position in the French aristocracy.

––⁓⁓––

Back in Chandernagore, Catherine's old ayah sat in the shade of the veranda and, by the length of that shadow, knew that by now Catherine was a wife. She knew little of the husband but had managed to find out his date of birth. Armed with that, and that of Catherine, she had paid for their horoscope, as would be expected in anticipation of marriage. In lugubrious tones the holy man had made it clear to her that Catherine and George's proposed wedding date was not propitious for their future together. However, as she knew Catherine would have dismissed such warnings as superstitious, she had not told her of the horoscope. Now her girl was gone, though, she brought to mind what else she had been told. It had sounded too fantastical, not unlike some of the Bengali stories she had plied Catherine with in her infancy. Perhaps it might come true. If so, then her young charge was destined for a remarkable life.

Calcutta

'Oh, no! You can't say that!' Fanny rocked back in laughter.
'*Pourquoi pas?*' Catherine giggled in return.

Fanny bent forward in mock seriousness. 'It simply isn't done, ye know!' and went on primly in her studied French, '*c'est un manque d'éducation,*' before again breaking into sniggers.

The two teenage girls enjoyed correcting each other's English and French respectively over their frequent breakfasts together. This was conducted on the veranda of Fanny's house on The Strand, Calcutta's main thoroughfare, a routine made all the more enjoyable by the attention they received from the passing gentlemen, Indian and European alike. For both girls had striking good looks, profuse auburn and blond hair respectively and a vivacity that seemed at odds with their surroundings.

Catherine dabbed a napkin at her lips and glanced at her companion who was carefully sipping her overfull cup of tea. She thought herself particularly fortunate in her friend Fanny Chambers. There was only a year or two between them and, both having much older husbands, they had quickly formed a bond based on their youthful sense of fun, not to say flirtation, as they found themselves flattered by the gallant attentions of so many gifted and experienced men of the world. Catherine had been brought up on the banks of this wide and sluggish Hooghly river which was home to a number of European settlements. Consequently she knew by sight, and was known by, any number of Dutch, French and British traders who spent their time travelling upriver to trade with their Indian counterparts in Murshidabad. Fanny had only recently arrived as a newly-wed, and her husband was similarly fresh to India. So she had found Catherine an invaluable friend as she grappled with this new way of life.

She had asked Catherine about how she had become George's wife. And Catherine was delighted to tell her: George Grand happened to be English but his fluency in French had given him an advantage over his fellow eligible Englishmen and she had come to look forward to his visits to Chandernagore. Apart from his amusing attentions, she had found he had a wider knowledge of local affairs than most of the young men she had grown up with in Chandernagore. Because, as she had told Fanny, he originally came out as a Company infantry officer and travelled the surrounding country before transferring to the administrative side as a Company Writer. He was more than *agréable*, he was a companion of wit and sensibility. She suspected Fanny was slightly jealous of their relationship and guessed Fanny's own marriage to her lawyer husband was more arranged than heartfelt. Whereas Catherine remained in regular contact with her father, she could not help but notice that Fanny's only mention of her father was merely that he used to be a sculptor of some renown. Even with the handicap of a mental translation, Catherine had noted the deliberate use of the past tense. It would be impolite to probe further and the young girls concentrated on their own friendship, fostered over this regular breakfast ritual.

The noise of activity on the river abated somewhat as the laborious work of the morning reacted to the rising heat of the day. The girls edged their chairs further into the shade of the overhead awning. We've been married a year already, thought Catherine. George was the best thing that had happened to her. She had been readily accepted into Calcutta society and together they had enjoyed the flattering attention paid to them as an attractive addition to the married expatriate community. Apart from George being valued by the Bengal Council for his experience, Catherine knew he was also her father's favourite son-in-law. Mind you, that was probably because she was his favourite daughter! George had similar tastes and they had together turned George's bachelor house into a more stylish home, relying on some imported French and English furniture but also locally crafted fittings and gorgeous Indian fabrics.

'So will you retire with George to England?' asked Fanny.

'Perhaps. If George wishes it,' shrugged Catherine. 'We are very comfortable here, of course, but I would love to see Europe. I have heard so much about it. My father still remembers France but I doubt he will ever return; he has spent too long out here. I do not want to spend the rest of my life in India. George's family is in London but he tells me he remembers it as more expensive than here, and not as friendly.'

'Oh, but you'll love London,' Fanny said, 'there is so much more going on there! Robert's friend, Dr Johnson, could not believe that we were prepared to leave it, so much does it have to offer!'

'Do you miss it?'

'Sometimes, but this is like a miniature London without the cold.'

For the senior ranks of the East India Company in Calcutta lived life to the full, possibly because of, more than despite, the high mortality evident all around them from the climate and consequent sanitary conditions. They held plenty of balls, masquerades, theatricals, concerts and the fashionable addiction to card play, especially in this, the cool season. None of this was strange to Fanny. For her part Catherine was familiar with the Bengal routine of breakfast parties, the afternoon siesta, changing to congregate *hawa khana* outdoors at sunset, dinner and then maybe changing again for whatever entertainment had been organised that night. Indeed both young ladies were looking forward to the ball being given that evening for the newly arrived Council member Mr Wheler, as Mrs Harriet Wheler was reputed to be as young and pretty as they.

Fanny picked up a fan as much to dispel the dust kicked up by the passing horses and tongas as to keep her face cool and free from perspiration. It was not only the climate that had surprised Fanny about India. She had asked about the status of Catherine's maid, a locally born Portuguese girl called Ana, and was relieved to hear she was a member of staff and not a slave. She had been shocked to find that, yes, slaves were bought and sold here by Europeans and Indians alike. Also that the men could be expected to have *bibis*, native mistresses, and would provide for them almost as family. Fanny admitted mistresses were not uncommon in English society, but was sure that they were less socially acceptable than she found in Calcutta. It was an education for them both. And Fanny was keen to learn. Catherine readily taught her the key Bengali expressions and what she knew of the Company's Council politics from George. She was proud that George Grand was part of the inner circle of Mr Hastings and Mr Barwell, all long experienced in the administration of the Company's Bengal Presidency. Whereas those Council members recently appointed from England, of which Mr Francis was the only original one to have survived, saw their role as to constrain the Council by regular disagreement. Or that is how George described it.

'Oh, but we get on very well with Philip,' interrupted Fanny. Fanny's husband, Sir Robert Chambers, had been appointed with Sir Elijah Impey, a school friend of Hastings, to set up the new Supreme Court in Calcutta. Robert had respect for Mr Hastings who had had the Moslem and Hindu laws translated and codified, but also found a good friend in Philip Francis, who had moved in the same London circles. Fearful of creating a divide, both ladies recognised their friendship would best prosper without reference to local politics.

Catherine was used to the close-knit community of Company expatriates, whether French or English, united in their determination to do as well as possible for the time they would spend in this host country. When the menfolk were not discussing business, they would refer to events and expectations 'at home' in Europe, an alien world to Catherine. There were times she felt like one of those rumoured upper-caste Indian wives, cut off from the world around them. But at least George encouraged her to enjoy all that Calcutta society offered. She would explain to him what Fanny had told her was suitably fashionable and he had readily ensured it was procured without concern for the cost. He was as proud of his stunning young wife as she was pleased to be so well looked after by him. If she stopped to think about it, Catherine believed they were admirably suited, a loving and lovely couple indeed.

The ball that evening was a typically extravagant event attended by well over a hundred of the great and mighty of the settlement. As the girls expected, most men had their more colourful embroidered coats and waistcoats and with fussy cravats rather than the plainer daywear, while the ladies wore their best hooped embroidered silk skirts and jewellery that sparkled in the candle and firelight. No sooner had Catherine arrived with George than Fanny borrowed her to meet the Whelers. Edward Wheler had not had time to adjust to Bengal and looked decidedly elderly (Mon Dieu, he must be over forty, thought Catherine) whereas Harriet Wheler looked the overawed teenager that she assuredly must be. Curiosity satisfied, Catherine and Fanny were about to move on when they were approached by an elegantly dressed gentleman, taller and thinner than most. Fanny introduced him to Catherine as Mr Francis, of whom, Catherine instantly recalled, her husband had such a low opinion. His wore a fashionably tighter fitting dark coat from which peeped his white shirt trimmings and cravat. Catherine put him as older than her husband but still this side of forty. He certainly was considerate and easy mannered towards her and not at all as haughty and obstinate as George had described him. Indeed, while many of the men were falling over young Harriet Wheler, Philip Francis was paying her more attention as the evening went on, addressing her in good, if somewhat English-accented, French.

Back at home, she remarked to George how gallant Mr Francis had been and George was not unduly surprised. 'He does indeed enjoy the company of pretty young ladies. It's a game you can expect him to play, with his wife and family thousands of miles away and someone as attractive as you here, my dear.' He smiled and added with a wag of his finger, '*Fais attention.*' Catherine was as careful as any young girl enjoying the attention of a suave and interesting man of means – for Philip's reputation at the card table preceded him – and, as Fanny playfully remarked to her, it was difficult to judge who was the moth and who was the candle. For, having not seen him until that ball, she now found he was often at the same entertainments they frequented and that it was not uncommon that he happened to be riding along The Strand whenever she was out in her carriage.

'Can you explain something to me?' Catherine asked Fanny. It had been puzzling her for some time that, while Mr Hastings may rule the Bengal Presidency like a nawab, able to make treaties, despatch expeditions, create legal systems and control the army, yet he was only 'Mr' Hastings and not 'Sir' Warren Hastings like Fanny's recently knighted husband, nor indeed born into the aristocracy which was the only path to such office in France.

'I don't know,' admitted Fanny. 'Perhaps we English just don't have enough aristocrats to go round,' she joked and then, stroking her stomach she added, 'but I'm doing what I can to increase them!'

Catherine raised an eyebrow '*Vraiment?*'

'Yes, really,' said Fanny. Catherine was both pleased and a little envious that her friend should be expecting a child. There seemed to be no reason why Catherine should not be in a similar condition by now. She had heeded all the advice of her old ayah and was as surprised as George that there was still no sign of their being blessed with a result from their passionate lovemaking. Still, at least she was able to continue to enjoy the continuous round of entertainments.

Some weeks later George came home from a breakfast meeting with Mr Barwell and told Catherine that Harriet Wheler had died the previous day. Catherine crossed herself with a silent prayer. Both of them were familiar with the risk to European newcomers of being struck down suddenly for no apparent reason. Some just did not seem to have the constitution to survive long. But it was still a shock that charming young Harriet should be here one minute and gone the next. They were both silent with their thoughts. Catherine remembered how well Harriet had looked at that ball, but also wondered what of hers might be available at the customary private auction.

George suddenly blurted out, 'I wish Francis would go as fast!'

'Is he ill?' asked Catherine.

'*Non, malheureusement.* He is a confounded nuisance.' Hastings was set on a reassessment of the land-revenue so that all classes were charged a fair and moderate rate and George had compiled the details for the Presidency Council to vote on. But Francis had objected and continued to undermine Hastings with contrary reports to London and encouraging dissent among the more influential Bengalis. 'He simply doesn't understand. This is a reform that will put money back in the peasants' pockets!' He started to explain it to her but Catherine found it sufficiently complicated to have some sympathy for Philip Francis. Still, she would be careful not to mention him in George's presence.

Fortunately George did not dwell on Council politics. When business required he would travel upriver, dropping off Catherine at Chandernagore to visit her family. Catherine always looked forward to this exchange of gossip and compliments.

'You've still kept your figure, I see,' her sister would say deliberately and Catherine would change the subject at that point. Her father was always interested to know how George was getting on.

'I would be sorry if you had to go to England, you know, but I would understand. Perhaps it would be easier for you to visit us in France by then,' he would say.

'Would the King let you retire?' she would ask, knowing that his dream was increasingly less likely to come to fruition. For the moment, her family was within easy reach and, if George and she eventually left wealthy enough to live well in Europe, then she knew her family would be happy for her.

—◊—

Catherine's mood tended to follow the seasons so that, when the annual monsoon arrived six months later, she was able to relax more as the temperature dropped to a more reasonable level. From under the cover of the veranda roof, she and Fanny watched the rain pelting the already sodden roadway, bereft of the usual busy traffic. It was a joy to smell again the clammy vegetation and listen to the constant drumbeat on the roof. Then, through the rat-a-tat of the rain, they heard the jingle of harness and shortly there emerged on The Strand a group of red-coated officers trotting by purposefully.

'Wonder what they're up to,' mused Fanny. The troop was shortly followed by a column of Company sepoys marching with musket and pack heading for the quay and whose officers also barely glanced in their direction. 'Something's afoot!' Fanny said looking towards the fort, from which another company of soldiers was leaving.

'A foot?' queried Catherine.

'Yes, and we'd better find out,' Fanny replied, motioning to the maid to remove the breakfast things. Catherine hurried home to find an anxious George waiting for her. Before she could ask him, he embraced her and said she must remain calm. For they were at war with France. He carried on in a rush, stifling her questions. It was to do with the French joining the

American rebels, recently successful at Saratoga, in making war on England. It transpired that the Council had just got the news from the new overland relay system via the Red Sea that Mr Hastings had established a year or so earlier. It meant that the French upstream at Chandernagore were almost certainly ignorant of the fact and the English could surprise them with minimum casualties either side. George assured her that they would be safe here in Calcutta. However, it was not Catherine's main concern.

'*Mais, ma famille!*' cried Catherine. George took her hand and soothed her as best he could.

'There's nothing we can do but wait. I'll let you know the moment I hear anything.'

She could not believe her family was now at risk because of the rebellion on the other side of the world.

'When did you learn this? Could you have warned them?' she asked George. He had only heard that morning as the Council had kept it secret until it had decided on, and marshalled, its military response. He shared her concern for their friends and family upriver, but expected a bloodless surrender given that Chandernagore no longer had the defences of the last war. Catherine struggled to understand how such unprovoked aggression could be justified.

George had explained to her that the East India Company did not answer to the British government and its officers held a Company rather than a King's commission. Surely, then, she asked, it could stay aloof from the national conflicts on the other side of the world? George thought it had been known to do so in the distant past but reminded her that the French in India were more directly servants of their King, as was her father, and were thus not in a position to be independent of its nation's hostilities.

It was a matter of taking the initiative before the French here responded to the declaration of war. Catherine was reminded how her family had been similarly expelled from Pondicherry by the English at the time of her birth, sixteen years earlier, but this was so unfair, so unexpected. She agreed with George that she should stay at home for the time being. He added, quite unnecessarily, that it would be best if she didn't speak in French to any strangers. Catherine had already resolved to only speak in English from now on.

It was a worrying time for them both, which obviously Catherine felt more keenly. Rumours abounded although there was an early consensus that Chandernagore had been taken readily enough. Eventually, they received news that Catherine's family, though dispossessed, were safe and unhurt. They would write again once relocated. The war preyed on everyone's minds. New battalions were raised for the Bengal army and a marine service was organised for the protection of the River Hooghly. George said both Francis and Wheler had typically condemned these precautions as utterly inadequate. Certainly the news from the Bombay Presidency was not good, but the success of the Madras Presidency in capturing the more substantial Pondicherry settlement raised morale. Friends visited Catherine again and she found the natural politeness of the expatriate community meant it avoided any triumphalism in its recounting the progress of the conflict to her. Later they heard that Spain had joined in the war, but that signified nothing in India and in no time Calcutta got back to normal business. Certainly the Indian traders were quick to recognise where their best interests lay.

'Normal' included the ongoing wrangle between Philip Francis and his fellow Council members. Philip never mentioned it to Katy, as he now called Catherine, when he met her at the occasional event, but George relayed enough for her to realise Philip's view of the various military exploits initiated by Hastings was entirely political. She continued to respond politely to him at their meeting, not least as he remained a close friend to the Chambers. Fanny was still very much her best friend. Fanny was a nineteen-year-old mother now, but her daughter was in the care of an ayah, which left Fanny free to resume her social life, though somewhat more seriously, Catherine thought.

Then, one December evening, when George had gone to dine with a friend, Catherine had gone upstairs to rest. She didn't undress as, she told Ana, she was waiting for George to return later that night. Lighting a candle, she heard a scraping on the balcony and a whispered 'Katy, Katy? I've come.' She quickly wrapped a shawl around her shoulders and crossed the room to find Philip at the top of a ladder perched against the balcony. She was shocked but he seemed to expect a welcome. 'I'm here. Ah, my Juliet. You look so lovely, such gorgeous hair,' he said as he leant towards her. She turned back but he grasped her arm. 'Such dainty hands,' he said as he made to plant a kiss on the hand.

The English came to her: 'What *are* you doing?' she exclaimed.

'But you said…' he began but was interrupted by a commotion below and Philip took a firmer grip on the ladder as it began to shake. 'Help me,' he said as it began to tilt and she reluctantly gave him a steadying hand as he came over the balcony. Ana's cries had brought help to the bedroom and before Philip had a chance to re-establish a dignified posture, the house jamadar burst in and seized him. 'Don't worry, mem'saab. I have him now,' he said as he pinioned Philip against the wall. The commotion downstairs had not ceased however and the sound of neighbours and staff vying for entry distracted the jamadar enough for Philip to escape his clutches and run down and out, pursued by his would-be captors or rescuers.

Catherine was still trembling when George returned in a hurry, summoned by another servant. 'Are you alright? What's happened?' She explained as best she could but he got a better report from the jamadar. He gave Catherine a hug and said, 'Thank God. You're alright now,' and continued to talk to her in soothing terms until he felt she had recovered enough to probe further. 'You're sure it was Philip? He didn't touch you?' and from concern he turned to fury, calling Philip words that Catherine had not heard before and vowing vengeance. He put his arms around her shoulders and led her back to the bedroom, which Ana had carefully restored to a more ordered condition. Sure enough the following day he had one of his military friends round – for George had kept in touch with his fellow Company officers after transferring to the civilian side – to serve a challenge to a duel on Philip Francis. Catherine was both shocked that the attempted seduction could lead to deliberate bloodshed but also inwardly thrilled that George would go to such lengths on her behalf.

'No, he did not touch me,' Catherine assured Fanny before the rumours started. Fanny was every bit as surprised and sympathetic as Catherine expected.

'I cannot believe it! What on earth made him do such a thing? Had he been drinking?' Fanny's shock was real. 'And George has challenged him to a duel. This is terrible! Philip is no marksman.' That seemed the least of it to Catherine, but she was able to assure Fanny that Philip had refused the duel. 'Can he do that?' Fanny wondered. 'Would George accept an apology?'

'No, that would be out of the question.' So one social crime had been compounded by another. It seemed all Calcutta was agog and Catherine found herself the subject of solicitous friends all keen, tactfully of course, to know the detail. She preferred to stay at home.

As a result she was still at home instead of her scheduled breakfast with Fanny when Richard Barwell called on George. She kept still so as not to interrupt them and couldn't help but overhear their conversation. Pleasantries over, George said clearly enough, 'I'm sorry, Richard, I tried but it didn't work.'

'So I gather. He will not fight?'

'No, I've tried shaming him into it but he is adamant that he shall not. He says nothing happened and so my honour is not impugned.'

'That a real pity. I felt sure he would.'

The exchange went on to other matters but Catherine thought hard. It was natural that George wanted honour satisfied but that phrase 'it didn't work' stuck in her mind. What didn't work? Was it his choice of challenger? She would ask George once he was free of his visitor.

A sneaking suspicion grew in her mind. The more she thought about the exact sequence of events, the more she felt that Philip had assumed he would be welcome. Why? She was sure she had been much less encouraging recently. Certainly George's reaction had been caring and protective. She needed to be sure and asked him cautiously, 'George, *Philip etait attendu, je crois*,' she ventured. 'I did not invite him. I don't know what gave him such an idea. You did not give him…' – she thought of the right word – 'some fallacious encouragement, did you?' George was shocked she should think so, and was quick to deny it. Something about the way he protested deepened her suspicions. Why would he invite a seduction? Catherine began to see the bigger picture. 'This challenge to a duel: You wanted a reason to call him out, to legally put him *hors du combat*, and you used me as… as bait,' she spat out the last word. 'How could you! This duel isn't about me at all.' She was furious.

George's denials became less strenuous. He spread his hands and added, 'You were not harmed. I made sure of that. Come, I would never let you be harmed.'

'How could you be sure? You do not care. All you care about is your idiotic Council vendetta.' And then another thought. 'Whose idea was this – Barwell's?' She could imagine that being the case.

Whatever George said only incensed her the more and, exasperated, he countered, 'Is this all the thanks that I get for being your husband, caring for you? And you're not much of a wife to me,' he yelled, 'you cannot even produce children!'

There was an immediate silence as they stared at each other. The unspoken had been spoken. Then Catherine said, 'I am leaving in the morning,' and went upstairs. He did not follow.

Chandernagore

Naturally, it was not as simple as that. George was waiting to greet her when she came downstairs the following morning and all for reopening their discussion in as diplomatic way as he could. But when he said how much he loved her, Catherine again lost her temper. 'How can you say that? You used me! I am not some tame pet you can do with what you like!' His remonstrations again served no more than to escalate the argument and she stormed out, scowling and heedless.

She talked it over with Fanny who was prepared to accept Catherine's analysis of the events and did ask tactfully if she and her husband could arrange a reconciliation for her. But Catherine was too hurt to consider it. They agreed she should stay with her family in Chandernagore for the time being and Fanny would seek to find out how intended, and how careless of the consequences, was this intrigue. So Catherine was collected by her elder sister, Marie-Anne, and her husband, Michel de Calnois.

'Can we just go now, please?' pleaded Catherine of her sister.

'Not until you tell me what exactly happened. It cannot be that serious!'

So Catherine went over how George had exposed her to rape just to trap a political nuisance to the Governor General into fighting a duel. No, she had not been harmed. No, she had not given the least provocation. No, George has made no effort to apologise and no, she could not stay a moment longer under the same roof. Marie-Anne conferred with Michel, whose reluctance to be involved was obvious. It seemed to make Marie-Anne more solicitous of her baby sister.

'Good, you can come and stay with us until this blows over. We will let George know where you are.' She motioned Michel to collect the bags and escorted Catherine to the waiting tonga.

On the way, Marie-Anne warned her that their father was staying with them, having been evicted from the Company's buildings, which Catherine was aware of, but that he was not at all well. This had happened to them before, just before Catherine was born, when the English took over Pondicherry. He had recovered from that then, but now, seventeen years later, he was not the same man. Indeed, he was not himself and Catherine should not expect much from him. It was not so bad for Michel who could carry on some trade on his own account with his usual Indian contacts, though when he needed credit to get the major contracts he had to act as an agent for the English Company, which was effectively the owner of Chandernagore. Or at least until a peace treaty restored it to France as had happened that last time. Catherine took little notice. She was just relieved to be looked after by her sister.

The Calnois home was not the same as when she and George had visited it before war broke out. Marie-Anne explained the surrounding untidy growth as the necessary lack of a gardener. Inside had a similar neglected look. Catherine began to feel guilty.

'I am so sorry to impose on you. I had no idea...' she said looking around. Her sister assured her she really was welcome and to make herself at home. Her father was genuinely delighted to see her and clearly had no comprehension as to why she should be there and without George, which was a blessing. He looked shrunken and his clothes looked shabby on him, though. Catherine remembered him resplendent in elaborate coat, colourful waistcoat and powdered wig, ready to pay court to the Nawab or to entertain the Governor. That was only a few months ago. Now, she took to sitting on the veranda with him and telling him about the Calcutta characters she knew. He would smile and nod occasionally but Catherine knew he was mentally locked away in a world of his own. Her sister was grateful for her company in that respect. Michel was busy negotiating the sort of deals that he used to delegate to others. Gradually, a routine was established and Catherine was even able to contribute from the allowance that George continued to give her. She wrote copiously to Fanny but it was some time before she got concrete news. She heard nothing from George.

The news she finally received from Fanny confirmed her worst suspicions. According to Fanny's letter, her husband, who was both a lawyer and a friend to Philip, had been told that George intended to pursue his attack on Mr Francis legally. In English law he had a right to bring a 'criminal conversation' action against Philip for the breach of fidelity with his wife. 'That's ridiculous. I am the injured party,' said Catherine, and carried on reading. It was not an unusual legal action among the English aristocracy with outrageous sums being demanded in compensation. It was clear that by this means Hastings – for he must be behind this – meant to beggar Francis. The delay in bringing the case to court was because Robert had advised

Philip to arrange for any key witness to be inaccessible as long as possible. Fanny added that, in her opinion, the reason George had not visited Catherine was so as to further justify the grounds for compensation. It seemed a poor excuse to Catherine and she knew George well enough that she doubted he was motivated solely to do his master's bidding. If it really did suit him to ignore her, she could be just as determined.

So the weeks passed in Chandernagore and Catherine was kept informed of the slow progress of the trial, not least from the scurrilous *Bengal Gazette* for which the case was a godsend in providing an ever-increasing circulation. Marie-Anne insisted on Catherine giving her a word-for-word translation, which served only to double Catherine's indignation. It seemed extraordinary to her that she was the only party not summoned to give evidence. Was it because she was only sixteen, or was it because she really was not the injured party? Even Ana, her maid, had testified to the events. And so it continued until a conclusion was reached just before the monsoon season. Adultery had not been proven and although the Court nevertheless found against Mr Francis, the damages were a fraction of what had been demanded. It was still a large enough sum when you considered Catherine had not been molested, said her sister mischievously. Catherine had to remind her that the point of the case was political, not criminal. And, as if to underline the point, she noted that Sir Robert Chambers had dissented from the judgement. Privately, she wondered if he did so out of loyalty to Philip Francis, or if it reflected his objective view on the justice of Chief Justice Impey's ruling. The whole legal proceedings were totally baffling. At least, if the paper was to be believed, the case had become a matter of public amusement, with even a witty little ditty by Col. Ironside doing the rounds. There seemed little sympathy for George. Certainly he made no effort to see her and the possibility of reconciliation, so much encouraged by her sister and brother-in-law, was lost.

At the end of the monsoon season, her sister bluntly asked, 'Is it not time you went home?'

Catherine had not given it much thought. 'You know I cannot go back to George.'

'Why ever not? Surely now the case is over, he is richer from it and in a mood to have you back?'

Catherine admitted what she held against her husband was that he had said she was no wife of his – not able to bear his children. It was different for her sister. Marie-Anne had lost children within months of giving birth, but at least she could have some. '*Mon Dieu!* You don't know what you are talking about!'

'Oh, I'm so sorry, it was stupid of me…'

'Stupid, no, you were never stupid. Selfish and stubborn perhaps,' she added, 'and vain. That vanity of yours will be your undoing.'

'I'm not!' Catherine actually stamped her foot. It reminded Marie-Anne of when they were younger.

'Oh you were always the spoilt one. It is time you grew up. You do not know how lucky you are to have got George and now you want to give him up!' Catherine was going to retort that it was he who had given her up but realised how silly that sounded. She resorted to sulking.

Catherine did wonder if it was the result of a secret prompting by Michel, when she then received a letter from Philip Francis. He apologised for putting her in the position she found herself in and, recognising her family's resources must be stretched, offered her the use of his cousin's bungalow further up the Hooghly towards the Dutch Company's settlement. It was a surprising but generous offer that Catherine discussed with her sister. Marie-Anne was all for her taking up the offer. 'But I do not know this cousin of his, Major Baggs, and surely it will implicate me with Philip Francis to a point they will believe I did encourage him!' Her sister pointed out that as long as the house was otherwise empty, who cared as to its ownership and, as for people believing her guilty of some relationship with Mr Francis, they were the sort of people who would have believed that irrespective of this offer. Catherine thought her sister was responding to Michel's wish to have his house more to himself, but then wondered if her sister wanted to be rid of a potential rival. Tut, she thought to herself, you are seeing ulterior motives behind everything these days. Here was an opportunity to be more independent again. Accordingly, she accepted.

Major Baggs's bungalow was a modest affair set back from the riverbank and looked after by an English-speaking retired sepoy. Marie-Anne had been able to tempt Ana away from whatever temporary work she had in Calcutta to re-join Catherine and the three of them made the Major's little holiday bungalow into more of a home. It was once again the cool season so that, from her new base, she was able to receive visits from the Chambers and one or two other friends. It was a relief to find she was still part of Calcutta society. It seemed George was less so and had accepted a job requiring much travel away from the Presidency.

It was only a matter of time before Philip himself came to visit his Katy. She recognised it was the price she must pay for the loan of the bungalow but she was not going to let him get off lightly. She did not invite him into the reception room but addressed him standing in the hall. Despite being half his age, she now felt more his equal and better able to challenge him.

'You have some nerve, sir! It is because of you that I am in this wretched condition. What made you think you were welcome that night?'

He intended to be contrite and confessed to being a fool that night, but was soon all too ready to suggest her present circumstances were more due to her husband's disproportionate reaction. He too had suffered as a result of those vile legal proceedings designed to humiliate him publicly and considerably more than was warranted. It was a conspiracy between Hastings and Impey and he would never forgive them for that. Realising his vanity was getting the better of him, he became more sensitive to her own position. 'I am sorry. I hope you do not find this humble bungalow too wretched though?' Katy was reminded she was in his debt and ushered him into the reception room and sat down, allowing him to follow suit. Politeness restored, they talked more generally and by the time it came for Philip to leave, he was able to express how grateful he was that she bore no ill will towards him, and that he wished to see more of her, if she would permit.

And so he did, and with increasing frequency. Catherine was unsure how to take his advances. On the one hand, she was flattered by his solicitous attention but on the other, she was not sure she wanted to give in to his obvious intentions. Fanny was no help. 'It's up to you. I would resist but then that is easy for me to say. If you really have finished with George, you cannot remain unattached for long. Just be sure of what you're getting into.' In the end Catherine realised she enjoyed having a hold on Philip and when the inevitable advances became more intimate, she responded. After all, it was not the lovemaking she had enjoyed with George. Rather, it was the clumsy satisfaction of a more superficial attraction.

Once it was obvious he was spending the nights with her, her sister was predictably angry with her. She told her in no uncertain terms that she had ruined herself and had no future. 'Do you think he will take you back to England and introduce you to his wife and children? How can you be so short-sighted!'

'What choice do I have?'

'There is always a choice! Everything that has happened to you here has been a result of your decisions.'

Catherine could only argue back. 'And what of your prospects, do you think you can go back to France after the war? Can you expect Michel's family to respect you without the wealth he was supposed to bring back?' It was a cruel exchange and Catherine showed her out, ashamed but defiant. 'I will show them!' She really did not know how, though.

There was little she could do. The situation was made worse when she received a formal letter from Major Baggs saying circumstances required him to sell up and leave India and the bungalow was therefore no longer at her disposal. She suspected gambling debts; it was not uncommon. Philip arrived almost as fast, aware of her predicament and quick to offer her and Ana rooms in his Calcutta home. It was indeed the logical conclusion to his careful wooing of her affections. So she returned to Calcutta with Ana. Here, Katy, as she now preferred to be called, was more obviously Philip's mistress and she was aware that, while he could take her to performances, she was not invited to more personal functions. But at least she had Fanny's friendship still and breakfast with her was a welcome break from looking after Philip's household.

She was also back in touch with the news. The war still raged either side of the Atlantic but, here in India, war with the Mahrattas in the West was over and the Madras President reported that Southern India would remain quiet. There even seemed to be a truce between Hastings and Francis, with Barwell retired back to England. But Katy had come to recognise the underlying enmity of Philip for the Governor General. In the evening he would pour out to her his bitterness over Hastings' policies and the inability of Council to appreciate his point of view. There were times, Katy thought, that she was seeing the mirror image of her dinners with George. Though George, she admitted, did not complain with as much vitriol as Philip did. She was used to providing a soothing distraction.

This peaceful interlude ended with the news that seventy-eight-year-old Haider Ali, with his French-led army, had invaded an unprepared Madras Presidency and beaten the Company's forces sent to stop him. Philip Francis had voted with the others to send troops and money to relieve Madras but was clearly agitated at this sudden change in fortunes. Katy realised that his taking it out on Hastings in the Council marked a more open rift between them. Consequently, she was not entirely surprised when Philip stormed home one day incensed that Hasting had insisted that the minutes reflect his view that 'Mr Francis was void of truth and honour', minutes which would eventually find their way to London. Katy was more surprised, however, that the provocation was enough for Philip to resolve to challenge Hastings to a duel. He spoke no more of it to her and, recalling his refusal to fight a duel the previous year, she hoped he had not meant it. After all, it was what Hastings clearly wanted and that was usually good enough reason for Philip not to. That was on Tuesday.

On Thursday morning, it was loyal Ana who woke her to say Mr Francis had left very early that morning having entrusted to her care a letter for her mistress should he not return. Horrified, Katy dressed hurriedly, asking the servants if they knew of Philip's destination. The household was dumb, stupefied even, and now aware of the life-or-death moment. She had no option but to wait. She returned upstairs, made herself more presentable and deliberately left his letter to her unopened hoping by doing so, she could render it unnecessary. Returning downstairs, she paced beside the front door, hands clasped tightly together, listening for anyone or anything approaching the house. Soon enough a young officer rode up and introduced himself as Captain Tolly. She composed herself as best she could, but it was obvious to the young man that she was aware of the situation. 'There's been a duel,' he hesitated unsure of her status, 'ma'am. Involving Mr Francis, ma'am.'

'Oh!' She steadied herself. 'I feared as much.' The young man had removed his cocked hat and fidgeted with it. 'How is he?' she cried, fearing the worst from his silence.

It was an awkward and unfamiliar situation for him. 'I don't rightly know. Colonel Watson was his second and brought him to my house. He says, although Mr Francis fired first, Mr Hastings was the more accurate and Mr Francis has a ball lodged in his chest,' he blurted. 'I can escort you there, if you wish?' Katy's mind was in a whirl, but she had enough sense to accept Captain Tolly's offer and he went to find a tonga for them.

They journeyed to Captain Tolly's house in silence while Katy regained her composure. Fortunately, Philip was alive though severely wounded. The doctor told her that he had done what he could: he had extracted the ball, cleaned and dressed the wound and it all depended on the next twenty-four hours. There was nothing Katy could do. If she would like to return home, he would ensure that she be kept informed of progress. Katy spent the time thinking how to plan for the worst but ended up without conclusion. So, it was a relief to her to be informed eventually that the wound was now unlikely to prove mortal, though obviously serious enough to confine Philip to bed for some time. Katy was happy to organise his staff and personally attend to the wound in the meantime.

Still, it was months before he was back to his old self, fulminating against Hastings and dictating letters to friends and family back in England to allay any fears and alarms. Hastings had been solicitous, making repeated enquiries of Philip's health, offering to visit. Cathy suspected he wanted to be sure of his work, but Philip stuck to the formalities in dictating his reply: he had 'a proper sense of the Governor General's politeness, but could not consent to any private interview', was how he put it. He would be seeing him soon enough at the Council meetings. In the meantime his Council papers were duly sent to him.

'Goodness, that chota peg tasted good!' Philip put down his empty glass and sat back on the divan. Katy noticed he still didn't use his left arm to adjust his position. 'Does it still hurt, then?' He confirmed his shoulder still gave him trouble if he worked his arm too much, but it was at least on the mend. It was unfortunate then, at that moment, he read the latest batch of papers brought that afternoon. 'Hell's bells and buckets of blood!' Philip jerked upright, causing him to further curse as his arm took the weight of the movement. 'The Governor General had been confirmed in his post for a further term! Have the Court of Directors lost their heads? It's Devaynes' work; he's always backed Hastings.' Katy was still trying to work out what bells and buckets had to do with it, but was left in no doubt that Philip's hope and expectation to that position now looked impossible. His friends in London had been unable to sway the Company directors back in London after all. 'Donc, there's always the Madras governorship, now that Whitehill has been dismissed,' suggested Katy.

'Be serious for a moment, please,' said Philip. 'The Madras Presidency is as good as crushed.' He looked so morose; Katy did not know what to say to cheer him. Philip shifted again on the divan and sighed. 'I have to resign; I'm finished here.' He looked despondent, but Katy was familiar with his mood swings. Surely his failure to oust Hastings wasn't the end of his career with the East India Company? She motioned for his drink to be replenished. Over it, he patiently explained to her just how much he was a lone voice in the Council: at best ignored; at worst emphatically contradicted by Hastings. Then there was the alarming losses in the South. As he had told the Council, British resources were already exhausted and the country was incapable of resisting a French invasion. There was no future for him here in India. His best prospects were back in England where he had the support of his friends and where he could best take revenge on Warren – bloody – Hastings. Katy did not care for this vindictive side of his nature, so different from the trouble he had taken over her. She could enjoy his protection and offer him sympathy but he really was getting disconsolate these days.

He winced as he sat further up on the divan. 'Would you like a hookah? I'm told it is very soothing,' she asked.

'No. I can't stand that rank tobacco smell,' he retorted. Katy suspected his refusal was more to do with his intent not to be seen to be going native. There were times he could appear more English than the other English. 'There's nothing for it; I'll have to go,' he finished as he drained the glass.

Katy crossed over to kneel by his couch. 'I understand. I will come with you,' she said quietly. Philip said nothing though and looked away. Katy sat up. 'But I cannot stay here; I have nowhere to stay.' Living with Philip had been accepted by their friends as reasonable recompense for how each had been treated but no one else could be expected to look after her in similar manner. Even her family, barely existing at Chandernagore, had since taken the view – what was the English expression? – that she had made her bed and must lie in it. Philip continued to look elsewhere as if marshalling his thoughts and then faced her.

'That's the point. You cannot stay here and you cannot come with me.' Katy wanted to demand the reason, though she feared she knew the answer. He was returning to his wife and children back in England, to job prospects that might depend on as good a reputation as he could purport. She could not fit into that future he planned for himself. She blurted out, 'What is to become of me?'

They discussed it over the following days and in the end he persuaded her that the only option was for her to go to France and start a new life, to be Mlle Worlée once more, and somehow put aside the last couple of tempestuous years. She may know no one there, but he could at least give her a letter of introduction to a banking family in Paris. She was young and attractive still and would soon forget him and her brief interlude in Calcutta society. For Katy, it seemed impossible and more designed to be a convenience to Philip, but she felt too drained to argue. Having come to this decision, Philip was determined to execute the plan as effectively yet smoothly as possible. She was resigned to let him organise everything and naturally he was content to pay for it and provide a line of credit to get her started. The following days he showed a willingness to get things done that had been absent from his Council affairs since the duel. She should travel with a maidservant – young Ana if she would go – and take a suitably neutral ship to avoid the risk of being caught in the current war with France and Spain. He was aware the Dutch East India Company – he referred to it by its initials, the VOC – further upstream at Chinsura, would be sending its merchantman home shortly. As each detail was relayed to her, Katy felt she should thank him but her overriding emotion was one of being abandoned, yet again, however gently he explained the logic.

At Sea

So it was that on a relatively cool October day Katy found herself deposited on the Calcutta quayside with a pitifully single travelling trunk, waiting for the hired bumboat to take her to the Dutch East Indiaman that had dropped sail in mid river for her. With her was Ana, who surprisingly had agreed to join her mistress on an adventure to a Europe that she too had never known. Philip was not there to see her off. He feared his wound would not stand the jerking of the palanquin, but they both knew a private parting could be better endured than a public one. There was no trace now of the tears of that earlier parting, not least because she wanted to put on a brave face for the only friends who had come to wish her bon voyage, the Chambers. Fanny was full of good advice and promises to write, but Katy's mind was numb. She had a last embrace from Fanny before she was helped down into the bumboat for the first stage of a journey far away from the only world she knew.

Once beside the merchantman towering above her, she took hold of the proffered boson's chair and, and with her ankles crossed and tucked as much to keep her balance as to thwart the boatmen's view from below, she was hoisted aboard. She looked with approval at the clean decks and fresh cordage of the Dutch merchantman while Ana was similarly hoisted to join her. They were welcomed aboard the *Zeeuw* (or *Zeeland*, she was told by the captain who seemed at home in a variety of tongues) and taken aft to be introduced to the other passengers who had gathered under a canvas awning to gaze at the English settlement with its massive fort. There were half a dozen men, all VOC employees of various degrees, and some of their womenfolk, all a lot older than Katy and Ana. They were most polite and having ascertained her husband was on Mr Hastings' staff, assumed she was returning to his family in England, and made no further personal enquires, a distancing made more natural by their limited English. It was a language barrier that suited Katy. Her little fists were taut on the rail as she watched Fort St George diminish behind them. 'I'll show them!' she vowed. 'I am not just some discarded toy!'

As the *Zeeuw* worked its way down the Hooghly estuary, her defiance mellowed into misery. She pondered her betrayal by first George and then Philip and how she had been let down by so many, even her own family. For days she nurtured her hurt and resented having to make this journey. Whatever her sister had said, her misfortune was the fault of others, was it not? Perhaps she should have swallowed her pride and been reconciled to George who at least would have looked after her. But Philip had shown such consideration; she really had had no option. It was Mr Hastings' fault that their relationship had to end. Yes, she was the incidental victim of Bengal's political feuding, or so Katy chose to view it, as she was transported to an uncertain fate. She stayed on deck to get the fresh breeze until, once past the Danish Company settlement to starboard, the *Zeeuw* finally reached open ocean at which point Katy had to surrender to that dreadful *mal de mer* that afflicted all those going to sea for the first time. As she staggered across the deck, it drove all other thoughts from her head.

Over the next three months Katy came to recognise the crew's routine and their masterful handling by the captain. Compared to them, she thought herself fortunate to be able to retreat to the passenger cabin while the elements drove the ship through the ocean. Once, during a calmer spell, she responded to the lookout's cry and ventured on deck to glimpse a sight of Pondicherry, the place of her birth, but it only depressed her to be reminded of her roots. Otherwise, driving wind and rain kept her below as they passed Dutch Ceylon and later the Isle de France. In the passenger quarters she whiled away the time improving Ana's French and comparing her limited knowledge of geography with her better-travelled Dutch companions. As they travelled ever south-westerly, they moved seamlessly from winter to summer and Katy's mood improved with the longer daylight hours. Her companions had explained it to her, but Katy just enjoyed the better climate and began to put those memories of an October Bengal behind her.

When she thought of her time in Calcutta, she no longer gave way to her image of being a helpless victim of circumstances and took heart, rather, in the knowledge that she should have more of an opportunity to create a new life for herself than either her family or indeed the disgraced Philip Francis. Her mood lifted with every nautical mile they journeyed away from India. Even the tepid sea spray thrown up each time the heavy merchantman crashed through the waves exhilarated her. She knew the purpose of the ship's various sails, sheets and instruments from her childhood dockyard trips but just how it all worked to keep them on course was not something she felt she needed to know.

Eventually, she learned that they were about to cross from the Indian Ocean to the Atlantic. After so many months at sea, everyone was on deck to get that first glimpse of their intended break on shore and the prospect of fresh fruit and vegetables. Sure enough, there was the tip of Africa and, as they came round it, they had their first view of Table Mountain wreathed in slowly melting clouds and with a host of masts jostling in the foreground. For this Dutch settlement was where the VOC fleet had rendezvoused and, as they neared the beach, she saw it was full of little boats ferrying goods and sailors to and from the bulky East Indiaman vessels in the bay. The *Zeeuw* passengers were landed on the wooden jetty beside a star-shaped fort, a tiny replica of Calcutta's considerably larger one, Katy noticed, as she staggered a bit while she got her 'shore legs'. Her fellow passengers had been before, of course, and a lady offered to show her the shops while the crew collected fresh food supplies. Katy was grateful for the opportunity to explore the town in her company, aware of the appraising looks she attracted from the many men that thronged this remote nautical staging post. Beyond the usual harbour buildings that she was accustomed to, the tree-lined streets were laid out in a formal grid with uniform clean white houses, each with a small set of steps to the door. It was a far cry from the hotchpotch architecture that she had been used to on the banks of the Hooghly. Katy watched carefully how her companion chose and paid for her wares. She was surprised there was no negotiation over the price, to which she was accustomed. So she did the same, in her case with sign language to the Dutch storekeeper and with a chit drawn on the VOC that the captain had thoughtfully provided her with. The dust of the streets swirled in the breeze and she did not wander far. There wasn't much to this settlement, realised Katy, and she had no regrets when it was time for them to return to the jolly boat that would reunite them with their East Indiaman.

'Is this the boat for the *Zeeuw*?' enquired a good-looking young man who had made his way along the wooden jetty behind a porter carrying a large portmanteau. He was well dressed with a satchel over one shoulder and an air of confidence that drew her attention. 'Jolly good!' he said as he paid off the porter and his portmanteau was stowed aboard. 'Anyone here speak English?' he asked as he made his way aft through the oarsmen.

'Yes,' Katy said and, after a pause, for she was not going to be Mlle Worlée again until Europe, introduced herself as Mrs Grand.

'At your service, ma'am,' he said with a broad smile, tipping his hat awkwardly as the boat rolled. 'Mrs Grand of Calcutta? I'm Tom Lewin, secretary to the Madras President.'

Mon Dieu, she thought, he must know all about me. But he was quick to change the subject:

'Which is my new home?' he asked her, pointing at the fleet of anchored Indiamen. 'I hope for a more comfortable voyage than that I've recently endured on His Majesty's frigate!' They fell to comparing politely their experience of much the same tempestuous monsoon that they had endured getting to the Cape. Once they were on board the *Zeeuw* and he had been introduced to their fellow passengers, they searched out a less busy area of the deck in which to continue their conversation. Looking across the bay, he explained how the British frigate that had dropped him off had had to return to the Indian Ocean station and he had procured a place on the *Zeeuw* as the last of the VOC convoy to arrive. But although Tom confirmed he was bound for England on Company business, he declined to elaborate. For her part, Katy answered that she was merely going to visit relatives.

'Mr Grand's family?' asked Tom, mock-innocently turning to face her.

Katy looked him straight in the eye. 'Perhaps, and how about you? Is there a Mrs Lewin waiting for you?'

'Goodness, no! I'm footloose and fancy-free,' he exclaimed. It wasn't an expression Katy was familiar with.

'What does that mean?' she asked, puzzled.

'Oh, only that I have no ties. Look, we're going to be spending another hundred or so days together. Can you call me Tom and I'll call you…?'

'Katy,' she smiled. They had plenty of time to work out their relationship.

The *Zeeuw* beat more steadily northwards in the weeks that followed and Katy was happy to spend more time with Tom up on deck. Certainly the off-duty crew had got accustomed to their two younger passengers spending time in a corner of the fo'c'sle where they could best avoid interfering with the ship's running. From that vantage point they would share with the crew the excitement of occasionally spotting other vessels from the convoy, though they had not the Company seamen's expertise in recognising each one by name. When there was mention of recrossing the Equator, Katy asked Tom, 'What day is it?' knowing he was keeping a record of their progress. 'I've lost all sense of time since Cape Town.' Indeed, she was conscious that time had been less of a factor in her journey while it was shared with him. He had proved to be very good company, intelligent and considerate towards her. He knew about the Francis trial from Hicky's *Bengal Gazette*, of course, but she was able to satisfy his curiosity sufficiently for him to avoid further mention of it. She learned that he too would rather put the past behind him. She knew his boss, John Whitehill, had been sacked for incompetence in the face of Haider Ali's offensive, but little else. She didn't fully understand his explanations but it was obviously important to him that he get his despatches to London to put the record straight. If that meant absolving Tom of any involvement with something suspect, she didn't press the matter. What mattered to the couple was the present, the close confines of the ship and their spectator role as it was trimmed for every change in wind to keep it in touch with the rest of the convoy. So they conversed on inconsequential matters, laughed at each other's errors in French or English and let their friendship develop to the amusement, if not envy, of the rest of the ship.

'What do you want to achieve?' she asked him once as they stood watching the wake of their vessel create bright shifting patterns through the undulating waves.

'Ideally I'd like to be governor of Madras,' he replied, 'what about you?'

Katy thought about the past distressing year. 'I want to be in control of my life.'

'Ah, we all want that,' Tom adjusted his hold on the rigging, 'but cannot do it on our own. We need the influence of others.'

'Influence?' she asked.

'Yes, we have to gain useful people's respect.'

Katy thought of Philip: 'Even if it needs a duel?'

Tom saw how the nearby sailors were watching Katy, 'Of course, pretty young girls have an unfair advantage in that respect!'

Katy was not to be drawn. 'What about luck, good or bad?'

Tom considered. 'I'd rather call it an opportunity or lack of it.'

'So London is an opportunity for you?'

'Oh yes, I hope so. And is Paris an opportunity for you?'

'Me too, I hope it.'

Then, a few days after they had passed the Canary Isles, they were alerted by the crew's excitement that something irregular had occurred. Their pace had slowed as the topsails were taken in and everyone was looking for'ard to where other convoy ships were gathering. As they neared, they saw a smaller vessel, with some of its sails in tatters, stark against the unbroken blue sky. Jolly boats were passing between it and the nearest East Indiaman. 'Something's a foot?' suggested Katy. Tom sought out one of the English-speaking crew but all he could tell him was that the damaged ship was the Dutch frigate *Den Briel* and that the wounded from an obvious engagement were being taken aboard one of the merchant ships. Signal flags were running up and down the ships and the crew of the *Zeeuw* conversed in small groups as each message was broadcast. Tom pointed out a jolly boat from the fleet flagship that was doing the rounds and he expected that they would hear more presently.

It was an anxious wait, but eventually they were summoned to the captain. They made their way through a silent crew to the captain's cabin. He looked up from the charts on his desk and motioned them to the two chairs facing him. He got straight to the point.

'We have learnt that England, your country, not content to be fighting the French, Spanish and Americans, is now at war with the Netherlands. In fact it has been since not long after we left Cape Town. Two of our frigates were sent to warn us and ran into a couple of English frigates. They beat them, naturally, though only the *Den Briel* has found us.' He paused to let the news sink in.

Tom and Katy were stunned. 'At war? Why for heaven's sake?'

The captain barely controlled his anger. 'It is well known that this convoy only makes this journey once a year, returning at this time fully laden from our East Indies with a rich enough cargo to keep our Seven Cities going. It has been the case for hundreds of years. I suppose it should be no surprise that England, doubtless short of money for its current battles, has chosen this moment to declare war on the Netherlands!'

Tom made to rise from his chair but then stifled his protest. None of them knew the full story and for the moment they were entirely in Dutch hands. He sat down again reaching out to hold Katy's hand.

The captain softened a bit. 'I'm sorry but your status has now changed and I must ask you to keep to your cabin and the poop deck for the time being.'

'But,' Tom said, 'we're no danger to you. Surely we can continue to move about freely?'

The captain was not unsympathetic. 'The *Den Briel* had many casualties. It is for your own safety that I ask you to distance yourself from my crew.'

Tom nodded. But Katy voiced their main concern. 'But you are still taking us to our destination, as was agreed?'

'That I cannot do. It is clear from the frigates' action that an English fleet lies between us and the Channel. There has been a conference on the flagship and we are now set on a new course.'

They got no further information from him and were duly escorted back to their own quarters. There they found the other passengers in heated discussion. They too were concerned about their new course and Katy understood enough of what was said to reckon that the fleet was making for Cadiz. She and Tom took to a corner where they conversed softly. 'Where is that?' she asked. Tom told her it was the main Spanish naval base and would be the centre of operations against nearby Gibraltar, if that had not already fallen. He feared it would not be the most welcoming of destinations even if their civilian status allowed them some freedom. Still, Katy could certainly become Catherine Worlée in order to complete her journey but Tom didn't see how he could get to England easily.

'Mind you,' said Tom cheerily, 'there is always the possibility of the convoy being taken by our fleet. I recall Admiral Rodney captured a Spanish convoy just before I left Madras.'

'Then you had best not throw your despatches overboard just yet,' retorted Katy. It was a subdued group of passengers who shared their next meal.

As the days passed and the crew showed no particular ill feeling towards their English passengers, they were able to roam as freely as they had before. However, the mood was very different. There was more attention to the horizon and outbursts of ill temper from a crew as concerned about their delayed pay as for the ship's safety. 'I had forgotten all about the war these past months,' mused Tom as he contemplated the end of their romantic cruise. He had, though, readily agreed with Katy that they should stick together once on shore and Katy had no trouble in procuring an interview with the captain. Tom didn't ask how she was thus able to retrieve the funds entrusted to the captain by Mr Francis on her behalf, but she came back with a small smile of success.

If Table Bay had appeared crowded, the bay of Cadiz was infinitely more so. It was clear that the port authorities were overwhelmed with the arrival of their new allies and there was much toing and froing of a variety of small boats and galleys among the massive Dutch merchant ships. The *Zeeuw* dropped anchor on the north side of the bay. As Katy had arranged with the captain, she, Tom and Ana were able to get a boat to ferry them across to El Puerto de Santa Maria opposite and well away from the Cadiz headland.

Once steady on their feet, Tom led them through the narrow streets away from the waterfront looking for suitable accommodation. Katy and Ana had trouble keeping up as they stared all around them at the magnificent buildings, churches and plazas, the like of which they had never seen before. Eventually Tom halted at what struck him as a coaching inn and arranged in French for a meal and a couple of rooms for the night. The three of them then sat down with relief to their first meal of fresh meat, fruit and vegetables for months. To complete the feast Tom had ordered a sweet wine they called 'Jerez', which went straight to their heads. It was with difficulty that they managed to get upstairs to their rooms. As Ana opened the door for her, Katy looked briefly at Tom and told Ana, 'You can have this room to yourself, Ana,' and followed Tom into the next room. When Ana awoke next morning, she heard through the partition enough to know that breakfast was going to be late that day.

Over another meal of enjoyably fresh and varied food, they confirmed their plans. Katy would accompany Tom to London. All the dread of the past weeks had been replaced with the exhilaration of a couple planning a honeymoon. Their best bet was to head for Lisbon where they could get a ship to England. They ventured into the town to better equip themselves for the journey as the clothes they had had since India had suffered from the long voyage and, in any event, they wanted to travel light. All three of them acquired workmanlike Andalusian garb and Katy piled her long fair hair up into a suitable wide-brimmed hat. It was Ana this time who roughly translated for them, hesitant about the locals' comprehension of her childhood Portuguese. For a sum that seemed exorbitant to Katy, they got places on the public coach north and exchanged the swell of the ocean for the buffeting of the road.

The coach deposited them in the Rossio, the centre of Lisbon, from which the paved streets were laid out in grid formation down to the magnificent Palace Square on the waterfront. It was a surprise to all three of them. All the buildings had a uniform restrained classical style in contrast to some brightly coloured tiled pictures on the walls.

'This looks brand new,' said Tom and indeed there was still building work going on away from the centre.

It was Ana who explained it: 'We were told of the earthquake that destroyed the city in my parents' time but I had no idea it was being rebuilt like this.'

Eventually, Tom found a shipping office and asked about a ship to England. The clerk snorted, 'Don't you know there's a war on!' The frequency of shipping to England was uncertain to say the least.

Katy was shocked at his rudeness, which Tom confirmed was more common in Europe than Asia. Eventually they learned that they could more readily get a schooner to Porto whence the Scottish companies would soon be shipping their port wine to England under a Portuguese flag.

They next visited the British embassy and received the latest information on the war: Lord Darby had relieved the siege of Gibraltar; there were gains and losses in the American colonies and a rich victory over the Dutch in the West Indies. Tom asked what had prompted England to include the Dutch in the war and was told their 'neutral' West Indies island had been a major supplier to the American rebels.

'So the VOC fleet was not the target?'

'Indeed not,' Tom was told. 'It was by chance that *HMS Flora* met the Dutch frigate and drove it south.' Katy showed her surprise. 'You may not have been at risk then, Mrs Grand, but,' he added with a smile, 'it is true their fleet would never have been allowed to pass through the Channel.'

What interested Tom more, though, was the news that Madras had been saved from Haider Ali by a relief force from Calcutta. It was cheering news and it would be a good time to be back in London. They were recommended a decent hostel and, glancing at Katy, a suitable dressmakers.

With another voyage pending, Katy despatched Ana for only a few specific extras for the journey. It seemed a long while before Ana returned to their lodgings with the requisite items and Katy noticed the blush in the girl's cheeks and a cheeriness in her manner that had not been evident since they had left Calcutta. Still, it was with some trepidation that Ana then asked if she could be released from Katy's employ. Katy readily agreed and when it became time to join the Porto-bound schooner, they parted with Ana on the best of terms. As Tom said, it would be better for Katy to have an English maid in England.

Porto proved to be a delightful break for just the two of them while awaiting a Bristol-bound vessel. It was as impressive as Lisbon but with a completely different and older baroque style. The young couple delighted in touring its streets and markets, finding English was readily understood by the traders and café staff. It seemed Tom was being taken frequently for one of the many British wine merchants that lived in the city. Katy thought how easy it would be for them to settle here if only he did not have other priorities. But he did. Eventually they were back at sea and on their way to England, the country to which Calcutta society had constantly referred and about which Katy knew nothing.

London

What would Fanny think of this? thought Katy, as she looked at herself in the mirror, removing the fichu from around her shoulders so that her hair tumbled onto her bare chest. She had worn lightweight muslin gowns in Bengal and was pleased to find them here in London too. The dressmaker had said this *chemise a la Reine* was the latest fashion and it certainly suited Katy's slim twenty-year-old figure, even if it barely kept out the chill. She was grateful for the woollen blankets that she and Tom nestled under each night. She went over to the window and watched the rain falling on the pavement outside. She would need her coat and hat to go out this afternoon. It had taken her time to get used to the London weather. Back in Bengal we used to enjoy the cool season, she mused, but here it was the least cheering time of year and she looked forward to the spring and some relative warmth.

She and Tom had arrived in London in the autumn after a brisk journey by coach from Bristol, and he had leased one of the new town houses on Russell Place, hired staff and introduced Katy to a different way of life than she had been used to. It was useful to have staff who knew their business but she was conscious that the more she relied on them, the less independent she felt. The daily pattern of meal times was as different from that in India as was the usual diet. In no time Katy was introduced to the typical English fare of red meat and white cheese, of milk and toast, and she learnt from the cook that that there was no embarrassment at procuring smuggled tea and sugar at an affordable price. If there was anything Katy was unsure of, she would think to herself: What would Fanny have done? It was not long before she had the respect of the staff and she and Tom settled into the routine of a typical married couple of means.

Tom had written to his parents from Bristol advising them of his safe arrival but they had not rushed to visit him. She knew his relatives would not approve of his taking up with a married woman and would prefer him properly married and with an heir or two, but Katy was *Mrs* Grand and nothing could change that. Tom had immediately visited the East India Company's head office in Leadenhall Street to explain the loss of despatches and register his interest in a fresh position in India. He found them more interested in the whereabouts of his former patron, John Whitehill, than in his own misfortunes. It seemed Mr Whitehill had no more returned to England than Mr Francis. Tom learnt that Philip Francis had indeed left Calcutta not long after Katy but had, at his own request, been dropped off at Ascension Island. Probably his wound had not coped well with the voyage, suggested Katy. In any event, that island was sufficiently remote that it would take him some time to find a ship to complete his journey.

Anything they needed was within easy walking distance and Katy was surprised to find there were English beggars and drunks in the streets and that they were tolerated. Generally she and Tom could make their way safely past such hazards, though Katy noticed the width of most of the streets meant horse-drawn vehicles tended to be purely commercial ones. She did notice a few shortened palanquins, which Tom advised her were called 'sedan chairs' and hired more for privacy than comfort. Apart from the markets, Tom had spent these winter months cautiously introducing Katy to the London sights, the concerts and the theatre. They were both new to this city and aware that only eighteen months previously the mob had taken over whole streets, looting and burning certain wealthy properties for weeks, which had been reported in India as the 'Gordon Riots'. Currently, though, it was the war that was the cause of popular discontent. From the newspapers available at his Club in St James's Square, Tom was made well aware that, after the fall of Yorktown that autumn, public opinion was noticeably hostile to continuing the war against the thirteen colonies for a further, seventh, year. The traditional enemies, Spain and France, were a different matter, however, and news of every victory or setback was greeted with howls of glee or outrage accordingly. The public executions at Tyburn were popular with Londoners but Tom was shocked to hear that some 80,000 had recently attended the particularly gruesome execution there of a Frenchman for treason.

So Tom and Katy planned their London excursions carefully and only gradually got to know its attractions. The square known as Covent Garden was particularly busy with taverns, shops and the nearby theatres. Katy would take Tom's arm and they would mingle with the other Londoners there, Katy paying particular attention to what ladies of quality were wearing, while Tom steered her through the jostling throng. There was no question that they made a handsome couple and while Katy kept close to him for fear of the reputed pickpockets, she noticed he had a certain swagger to his stride as they explored the area. Tom had heard a new print shop had opened in Drury Lane and they joined a crowd gathered there to see what it had to offer.

'But they are all of ugly people badly dressed,' she said of the pictures displayed in the window.

'They are meant to be. It's an exhibition of caricatures,' Tom tried to explain.

'But people buy them?' she asked incredulously.

'Well, Mr Holland hopes so,' said Tom reading the name over the door. They walked down to Charing Cross where Katy noticed a shop selling maps and was fascinated by the ones displayed in the window. They entered and Tom ended up buying a large scroll which they took home.

He spread it out on the floor, anchoring the corners with whatever heavy objects came to hand. 'This is Europe,' he told her. He pointed out Cadiz and Lisbon and, with a finger on London, told her that was where they were. He pointed again: 'This is France. Where does your family come from?'

'My father told me, but I forget. It did not mean anything to me. Where does your family come from?' Tom pointed to somewhere in the middle of England. 'And will you go back there?'

'I doubt it. I hope that, working for the Company, I can afford to retire to a better place than that.' Katy understood. It was same ambition as of the Frenchmen working for the *Compagnie des Indes*. She had noticed how similar the houses on Calcutta's Strand were to the better ones on The Strand here. 'Is the Thames like the Hooghly?'

'Not really. It's tiny in comparison. The Hooghly is part of the estuary of the river Ganges, as you know.' He leant over the map. 'The nearest equivalent is the Rhine,' and he traced it on the map, 'and Antwerp here is the equivalent of Calcutta.'

She pointed at the different shades around it. 'And different countries are along it, as in India?'

'Well, sort of. This is Holland, where the *Zeeuw* was bound. Belgium here is part of the Austrian Empire controlled from...' his finger made an arc over to Vienna, '... here. And some of the states along the Rhine are controlled by Prussia...' another arc, this time to Berlin, '... here.'

Katy looked at him propped up on his elbow. 'And this part,' she said, putting a finger on his forehead, 'is controlled from...' her finger arced downwards, '... here!' They laughed as he rolled over to her and took her in his arms.

—⁓—

Tom had independent means; that Katy knew. But those means were not unduly generous, which is why Tom had joined the East India Company in the first place. He made frequent trips to his Club as much to check market prices and gossip as to catch up on the latest news. It was shortly after Lord North had resigned and a new Whig administration had been brought in that Tom returned home with a companion.

'Katy, my darling, let me introduce you to Alan Fitzherbert, my friend from Eton.' Katy took note of the elegantly dressed young man with a narrow face and piercing eyes.

'Enchanted,' he said smiling broadly at her. 'It's a pleasure to meet a young lady that Tom thinks so highly of.'

While they took off their coats and hats, Tom told her how he'd run into Alan at Lock's in St James Street, the first time they'd seen each other for years. Invited to sit down, Alan then explained he had only just come back from a posting to Brussels at the request of the new government. He too was unfamiliar with London but had got to know the area around Brooks' Club, which was how he came to run into Tom. It was obvious to Katy they were old friends and could talk together for hours, but Alan was considerate enough to include her in the conversation about the London that they had explored so far. In no time though they were talking about the new government and the prospects each of them might have once an end to the wars had been negotiated. Katy was pleased to note that Tom referred to 'we' rather than 'I' in this context. Katy was happy for him and rather hoped his friend Alan could anchor Tom more to London now that it had become more attractive to him. So, when Tom received a summons to East India House in the City, Katy viewed it with less enthusiasm than did Tom. 'At last, they may offer me a position.' He blew a kiss as he left.

It was a different Tom who returned. Noting his sombre mood, she got him a glass of port and waited for his explanation. 'Sorry, Katy, but it's that damned Whitehill business. One of the Company's ships, the *Osterley*, was taken last year by the *Elizabeth*,' – he pronounced the name in French – 'and the directors now believe it to be John Whitehill's.' Katy's puzzlement was obvious. He carried on more slowly by reminding Katy that the French in Pondicherry were the most significant element of the *Compagnie des Indes* and that, before the war, the Madras Presidency did a lot of business with them. Among other things, John Whitehill had commissioned a new merchant ship, the *Elizabeth*, in partnership with one of the French Company's officials to carry their private trade back to Europe. When war broke out, Tom believed John had sold out his share to the French partner. Tom left the drink on the table and stood up to pace the room while he went back over the interview. 'Apparently the French then equipped it as a privateer and it was that warship that took the fully laden *Osterley* worth some £300,000.'

'But that's not Mr Whitehill's fault, surely,' said Katy.

'It all depends,' said Tom, 'if, or when, John sold his share and, as the directors pointed out to me, if the deal included his share of the prize money. Prize money from the loss of an English Company ship.'

'Oh!' she said. 'But you know, don't you?'

'I'm not sure. But I do believe John didn't gain from that action at all. But any proof lies at the bottom of Cadiz Bay. The directors have only my word for it and clearly doubt me.'

'But why?' Katy's confidence in Tom was total.

'Because, according to the *Osterley* captain's report on his release – which is what has prompted this late enquiry – the *Elizabeth* initially flew the correct British signals, and only John and I should have known those. There could be another reason for that, of course, but the directors want some recompense for the loss and rather hope to get it from John.'

'Do you know where he is?' Katy asked.

'I suspect he's in France,' replied Tom. He explained further. The French officials at Pondicherry had also provided banking services for some of their English counterparts. As the East India Company now forbad its servants to send significant sums to England in order to protect the liquidity of their Indian operations, certain of its officials had used the *Compagnie des Indes* to send their money to France from where it could be collected once they had returned to Europe. As a result a certain Monsieur Perregaux was banker to a number of influential Company men. The war would have made it near impossible for them to draw on their funds in France, but he suspected Mr Whitehill, with his *Compagnie des Indes* contacts, had succeeded.

Katy was learning. 'Do you have funds there, Tom?'

'Sadly, no,' he smiled. 'You have to have made a lot more than I ever did to make it worthwhile!' The Frenchman's name, Perregaux, sounded familiar to Katy. Yes, it was the name of the banking family that Philip had referred to when offering her a contact in Paris.

Katy learned a lot that day but found she was not unduly shocked. Her exposure to the expat society in Calcutta had made her aware that the prospect of making more money than they might in their home country had made many of them more self-assured certainly, but also less scrupulous. She thought of the relative ambitions of George and Philip and concluded with relief that she now had Tom. As spring turned to summer, so their social life improved. Katy was much admired by their new friends from Alan's circle, who nevertheless respected her as Tom's consort rather than some temporary doxy of his. There was no shortage of invitations to join them in attending the favourite public performances. Thus Katy was introduced to Shakespeare's *Romeo and Juliet* (although Tom told her afterwards that Mr Garrick has changed the ending) and Sheridan's *School for Scandal*, which had Tom amused and Katy confused. On the other hand she was fascinated by Noverre's ballet at the King's Theatre, a completely new form of theatre for both of them.

Tom enjoyed widening Katy's knowledge of affairs. When news broke of a significant naval victory in the West Indies, Tom explained the effect on the cost of sugar and tobacco. He ventured to further explain how the reduced prospect of France winning the war was reflected in British government loans being at only 3% yield while those of the French government rose to 6%. It was heady stuff, but Katy loved his confidence in her ability to assimilate it.

Alan had asked her one time whether she minded their celebrating French defeats. She had had to think about it. She was French but not from France. When she married George she knew she became English but somehow that hadn't mattered then as they were all part of an international expatriate society. She had lost touch with her family in Bengal whose last desire had been that she had better be the responsibility of Philip Francis. No, she had no strong affinity for France, or indeed to George, still legally her husband, for that matter. Her loyalty was to Tom. Alan had nodded sympathetically and changed the subject.

Then, one morning, Tom received a summons to attend a House of Commons Committee set up to investigate the Madras Presidency's handling of the invasion by Haider Ali the previous year. Tom did not reply to it, telling Katy that he was aware that Parliament was antagonistic to the East India Company and was looking for any excuse not just to criticise it, but to further interfere with its running. If he was to obtain his next position with the Company he needed to avoid being cast as 'the witness for the prosecution'. Katy may have been content for Tom not to get a post just yet, but she shared his concern for his reputation, especially when the summons was repeated a week later. Tom cancelled his usual whist evening and spent the time instead scribbling notes of what he remembered of the sequence of events and decisions taken in Madras over a year previously.

As luck would have it, the latest influenza epidemic claimed the life of the Prime Minister, which meant a new government would have to be formed. Whether it was due to the feverish lobbying for places in the new government, or a fear of the influenza, the members of that Commons Committee were sufficiently distracted to fail to follow up on their summons for Tom to appear. He and Katy, with the rest of the British public, waited to see who would be the next Prime Minister. Eventually, the King reluctantly appointed the Earl of Shelburne as head of the new government, the third that year and again without a general election. Once that was settled, Tom received a further summons to attend the Committee with a strongly worded warning about the consequences of not heeding a Parliamentary enquiry.

Tom and Katy were still debating his response when Alan Fitzherbert was announced. They were all for sharing their worries but he was quick to interrupt. 'Forget about the Committee; I have a proposition for you!' He was pleased with himself and had good reason. 'Shelburne's new government has appointed me with plenipotentiary powers (Katy thought she had enough English vocabulary by then) to negotiate peace terms with the French and Spanish.' He paused for effect. 'And I want you, Tom, to be my secretary! It will mean spending time in Paris, but rest assured, the Exchequer has deep pockets to get this satisfactorily concluded.' Tom was eager to accept; he had nothing keeping them in London. Quite the opposite, it would release him from the Madras enquiry. Returning to the role of private secretary was a fortuitous opportunity and he was flattered Alan had confidence in his abilities as much as confirming him to be a good friend.

Naturally Tom wanted to know more about the negotiations. Alan would be taking over from Thomas Grenville, the previous government's representative, whom they should first meet before engaging with the French and Spanish representatives.

'But doesn't this require us to deal with the Americans too?' Alan explained that an expert on America, Richard Oswald, would be negotiating separately with the Americans, which was the tougher negotiation, but that Grenville had already managed to divorce the two issues on behalf of the previous government. Alan sketched out the likely motives in the negotiations. The French would be the main contender:

'We want our West Indies back and they'll want their East Indies back. You, Tom, know more than most about their East Indies. We control the oceans now too. We hold a good hand.'

Katy interjected, 'And French bonds are at 6% so they must be having more difficulty financing the war by now than us.' Both men looked at her with some surprise.

'We have copies of Necker's report on France's finances, which show a remarkably healthy position,' said Alan deliberately, 'but you're right, the stock markets generally know more about the reality than governments profess. Yes indeed, that's significant.' She smiled. She wasn't just a decorative ornament! Alan looked at Tom who nodded in understanding as Alan turned to Katy and told her in his now familiar decisive manner. 'You're coming too, of course, Katy. We need you on the team.' He did not explain quite what for, but that did not worry Katy a bit. Even if it was only to manage their household, it would be more purposeful than staying in London waiting for something else to come up. Katy had difficulty concealing her excitement. Forget Madras, she was going 'home', as her family had referred to France. And as one of an important diplomatic entourage. She would make herself useful and show them she was worthy of their trust. Alan's French was fluent from his time in Brussels and Tom's French had improved as a result of Katy's informal tuition on the *Zeeuw*. None of them spoke Spanish but it was assumed the Spanish representatives would converse in French, not least because the negotiations were being held in Versailles.

The two of them continued to discuss the bounds of Alan's remit while Katy mused on what she should wear for this expedition and whether Paris fashions were the same as London ones. Alan summarised the Spanish situation. They held Menorca and Florida and wanted Gibraltar, which was still holding out. 'We want Menorca back,' advised Alan, 'but the loss of the American colonies makes Florida of less concern to us. We'll be liaising with Richard Oswald over that.' As for the Dutch, they would want Ceylon back but the French had occupied that at the moment anyway. The discussion eventually began to tire. The candles were low and the bottles were empty but there was one last question for Alan: 'When do we leave?'

Paris

It had taken time to arrange passports and correspond with the various interested parties ahead of their passage across the Channel. However, they eventually arrived in Paris and established themselves in Grenville's former residence there. Katy's first impression of Paris was that it seemed older and more cramped than London. 'That's because it never suffered a Great Fire as we did,' explained Tom. He accompanied Alan to present their credentials at Versailles while Katy organised the household. Tom and Alan had brought their own valets and a young relative as a confidential courier from London while the rest of the staff were Parisians, including the cook who had refused Grenville's handsome offer to move to London. I need a maid too, thought Katy as she struggled to get a brush through her thick fair hair. Katy was soon besieged by suppliers demanding repayment of what struck her as highly suspect debts apparently incurred by Grenville. It took all her limited Bengal experience to negotiate settlement, while resolving to find alternative suppliers in some instances. Grenville's Sèvres porcelain had to be replaced and the cellar was woefully short of good vintages. Alan had also charged her with reading the daily *Journal de Paris* and passing on any news of the war, politics and economics. The newspaper had duly reported on the arrival of Mr Fitzherbert as King George's new representative and, as Alan had predicted, there were any number of invitations from would-be interested parties as a result, to which Tom drafted responses according to Alan's rapid dictations.

Tom and Katy's arrival had not been published. So Katy was surprised to receive an invitation addressed solely to 'Mme Grand'. It turned out to be from Mme Adelaide Perregaux who had an address to the north-west of the city in the Faubourg Montmartre where the air was healthier away from the crowded city centre with its smoke and smells. Same as London, thought Katy, recalling Russell Place. Tom was equally intrigued but it was on her own that Katy took a cabriolet to rue du Sentier, off the Boulevard Poissonnièrs. Although the street was narrow, the buildings had a relatively recent, classic look. Admitted to the Perregaux house, she found the interior lavishly but tastefully decorated. Katy put Mme Perregaux as not much older than herself, maybe in her mid-twenties, with a sparkle in her eyes and fashionably dressed, with a bunched lace neckerchief over the top of her gown. She introduced herself as Adèle and welcomed Katy as Catherine in French. It was the first time Katy had spoken at length in that language for a while and it took time to relax in the company of this vivacious lady who was all for telling her which Paris landmarks she should visit, and indeed whom she could recommend as a suitable lady's maid. The point of the invitation was revealed, though, when she introduced her husband, Jean Perregaux. He was older, probably in his forties, and quite soberly dressed, which belied his cheerful, expansive manner. He was delighted she had come to Paris as Monsieur Francis had written telling him to expect her. He understood

M. Francis to be now in London – *en famille*, he stressed – and looking to acquire a seat in the House of Commons. Clearly, Jean Perregaux was well informed and knew enough about her reason for being in Paris.

When Adèle left the room on some pretext, he leaned towards her, saying he had a confidential matter for her attention. Catherine was immediately on her guard, but he reassured her. He told her that, as a banker, he had money on her account entrusted to him by Philip Francis. Katy couldn't hide her surprise. He told her the sum and offered to continue to be custodian of her account if she wished. '*Un compte bancaire de ma propre?*' This was incredible. It wasn't much, enough to have tided her over had she arrived on her own, but no married woman she knew had her own money. She silently thanked Philip and begged forgiveness for all the bad thoughts she had had of him since leaving Calcutta. She signed where indicated. What would have happened if she had not come to Paris? Then, Perregaux replied, he would have assumed she was sufficiently settled as to not need it and it would have reverted to M. Francis's account. Adèle then re-entered, doubtless on cue, and expressed the hope that she and Tom would be happy to join them for dinner soon and be reacquainted with Mr Whitehill and some other people they would find interesting. It allowed Katy to report to Tom that she had been invited to sound out his interest in being reunited with John Whitehill, without mentioning her remarkable gift from Philip Francis.

Not long after, Tom and Katy were invited by the Perregaux to a musical soirée followed by dinner. They were introduced to a range of characters, whether as friends or clients of Jean Perregaux, they could not be sure; probably both. John Whitehill was there as expected, as was another authority on India, a

Scotsman called Quintin Crauford with his Italian mistress Eleanora Sullivan, among others of the international Perregaux circle. After the briefest Latin grace, Adèle Perregaux announced to the assembled diners that there would be no mention of politics at her table. She need not have worried: the gentlemen were clearly more interested in Tom's consort than the role that brought him to Paris. Katy found herself being addressed by a Prussian diplomat on the one hand and a well-known actor on the other. She found it difficult to keep up but was pleased to note that Tom was increasingly relaxed in this company.

Throughout these summer months both Tom and Katy were kept busy by Alan. Tom drafted regular despatches for Shelburne and made occasional enquiries of the relative commercial worth of various far-flung islands on Alan's behalf. While Katy passed on whatever was of use in the newspapers, Tom frequented the cafés, a very masculine environment, for the sort of news that she could not find in the newspapers and would return full of tall tales of scientific discoveries and extreme politics. It was a welcome distraction from the serious discussions that Alan would require of them. Already, Alan had agreed with Richard Oswald that peace with the Netherlands would be linked to the American negotiation. It left Alan focussing on the Bourbon Alliance of France and Spain. At first Alan would voice his frustration.

'The trouble with Vergennes and Aranda is that they are not used to having to deal with a gentleman half their age.'

'At least they are totally trusted by their monarchs,' said Tom, 'which is more than can be said of Shelburne.'

'True, and Vergennes doesn't have a Parliament ready to pounce on the slightest concession.'

Later they came to appreciate that, for all his dislike and distrust of the British, Vergennes was efficient in dealing with each point of the negotiation. Progress had been steady through the summer months while the Duc de Crillon, the victor of Menorca, was bringing the largest concentration of French and Spanish forces of the war to bear on Gibraltar. The engagements in America seemed small in comparison. In Paris, Tom and Katy had only to go to the theatre to find the audience regaled with demonstrations of the coming attack. But the outcome of the siege had yet to be determined and Alan discussed with Tom the value of aiming to strike a deal with the French before, and separate to, one with the Spanish.

These serious considerations apart, Tom and Katy were able to enjoy Parisian entertainments, often in the company of others of '*le coterie Perregaux*' as they came to regard that group. Quintin Crauford and Eleanora were particularly good company. While Tom was fascinated by Quintin's encyclopaedic knowledge of art and literature, Katy enjoyed modelling herself on Eleanora's unassuming yet stylish manner. It was Eleanora who introduced Katy to the fashionable Grand Mogol dressmaker's shop on rue du Faubourg Saint-Honoré, though Katy was horrified by the prices and resolved to stick to the new arcades of the Palais Royal for less expensive though no less fashionable dresses, shawls, shoes and hats. She introduced Tom to this redevelopment and when she later visited a hair salon there, he must have spent some time in a jeweller's. For it was not long after that he presented her with a present.

'But it is not my birthday, Tom!'

'Does it have to be for a birthday? This is a reminder of something we share,' and inside she found a charming silver chain and pendant of a sailing ship inset with a couple of diamonds. 'It's beautiful. Exquisite. We are the diamonds on the *Zeeuw*?'

'Assuredly so,' he said with a grin.

'Oh, thank you a thousand times. How clever of you, Tom!' And Katy immediately put it on.

It was rare for the two aspects of their life in Paris to conflict. Jean Perregaux had worked for the former finance minister, Jacques Necker, who lived round the corner in rue de Clery, and Jean had expressed the general mood that he should never have been dismissed. He explained that France was at war without raising taxes for the first time and that had made Necker very popular. So he could not understand how he could be replaced by a thirty-one-year-old, to which Tom admitted his own finance minister, Pitt the Younger, was only twenty-three. '*Touché!*' It was the nearest Perregaux came to talking politics with Tom. Tom was aware that the major campaign planned for Gibraltar had been financed by this youngster's State Lottery, but he was surprised to be told a week or so later by Katy that she had happened to overhear that the proceeds were going rather to supporting the Exchequer, *La Caisse d'écompte*. 'They *must* have a liquidity problem,' Tom reported to Alan.

Another of that coterie was one of Perregaux's neighbours, Elisabeth Vigée Le Brun, Adèle's contemporary, who had already established a reputation as a portrait painter. It was her portrait of the Queen that had set the fashion for the *chemise a la Reine*. Consequently, she was never short of customers whom she charged over 2,000 livres for a portrait. At which sum, Tom shook his head at Katy and they both laughed at such extravagance. Katy was impressed by the fresh, somewhat sensual way Vigée Le Brun portrayed her female subjects and could understand how she had become the first woman member of the *Acadamie Royale de Peinture* against all that male opposition. 'About time,' Tom remarked, 'I believe there have been lady artists members of our Royal Academy from the start.'

Katy punched him lightly 'You can be so...' she looked for the right word '... so English!'

'That's what I'm here for,' he smiled.

Towards the end of September everyone in Paris was desperate to hear the outcome of the Grand Assault on the Rock. 'London is no better informed than us,' reported Alan. He knew that the success of his mission depended on Gibraltar surviving this major offensive by land and sea. If so, the French and Spanish would have to agree his draft preliminary treaty. Then news began to trickle in and a hush descended in the cafés and kiosks of Paris. When the full story emerged, it was recognised that the attempt had been a bloody and costly disaster. Crillon, commander of the joint French and Spanish forces and hero of the Mahon siege, was being roundly blamed.

Katy learnt that nothing is ever straightforward in diplomacy. Months later, as the days became shorter and the weather colder, Alan was still pacing the room fuming that he could not get a preliminary peace treaty concluded. 'I cannot understand it,' he said, 'they know they have the only deal they'll ever get from us now and still they hold out. The latest delaying tactic is their fishing rights off America. I've referred that to Richard Oswald. There's something else, I'm sure of it.' Alan had been urged by Shelburne to bring the negotiation to a point that he could report favourably to Parliament. Alan worried that he was being asked to secure an agreement at any price. That had been the approach with the Americans; but he felt Shelburne should allow him to be more robust with the Bourbon representatives. Secretly, Tom and Katy were pleased with the delay as they could continue to enjoy the continual round of engagements provided by their new friends. While Alan spent a fruitless time pestering Vergennes and Aranda in

Versailles, Tom and Katy spent a carefree time enjoying Gluck and Grétry at the opera.

In the end it was the Americans who tipped them off, having problems of their own getting the Spanish to agree their treaty. 'I think,' ventured Franklin, 'that you'll find the terms of the Bourbon Alliance are such that France cannot make peace with Britain until Gibraltar is taken.' It seemed an unnecessary quibble to Alan since France had accepted the separate American treaty, the raison d'être of their participation in the war. But at least they had something to work on, and work on it they did. Tom was charged to return to London with a confidential proposal to offer a concession that should tempt the Bourbon Alliance to conclude the treaty and hopefully be acceptable to Shelburne who would have to sell it to Parliament and the King. Alan knew the Admiralty would never agree. That was for Shelburne to negotiate. 'I want you back here before Christmas,' Alan instructed.

Tom looked out at the snow flurries whirling along the Paris streets and confessed, 'There are times when I wish I was back in Madras.'

'That reminds me, Tom: here's a letter for that Parliamentary committee of yours. They should let you off with a token fine for non-attendance.' Thanking Alan, Tom was soon on his way.

In Tom's absence, Katy continued to frequent rue du Sentier and enjoy the company of the independent spirits that were cultivated by her banker, as she liked to think of Jean Perregaux. His dealings extended to correspondent banking partners in Hanover and Geneva. In his view, banking and the arts knew no boundaries, and the sooner the rest of the world took the same view, the better it would be for mankind. However, Adèle confided that Jean was getting worried at the falling value of his stock and hoped she, Katy, could bring them good news soon. Katy said she knew nothing more than what was reported in the *Journal de Paris*, which Adèle chose to believe. Selfishly, Katy thought no news is good news as she had begun to dread leaving Paris and parting with the lively coterie of which she and Tom were part. Tom had taken her to see Beaumarchais's play *The Barber of Saville* in London and she was delighted to be asked now to accompany Mme Fourniels, the aunt of one of the directors of the *Compagnie des Indes*, to a performance of his much-awaited sequel, *Le Mariage de Figaro*. Catherine, as the aunt called Katy, was fascinated and thrilled by this satire mocking the immorality of the aristocracy. In turn Mme Fourniels was pleased to have such an agreeable companion and suggested Catherine join her for other staged events.

Tom returned before the month end and was immediately closeted with Alan for some time. He later confided in Katy that he had had a hard time convincing Shelburne that their proposed Crillon face-saver, as he called it, was the only way to break the deadlock. Initially Shelburne had considered that the offer of Menorca to Spain too much of a concession, but eventually he agreed that it should be enough for the preliminary treaty to be concluded, regardless of Gibraltar being British still.

'But would they trust you to still hand over Menorca once they'd signed the treaty?' asked Katy.

'We're hoping they have to,' Tom said with confidence. 'We also have to hope Parliament will accept such a concession.' For, as he told her before joining Alan on the onward journey to Versailles, the latest he'd heard before leaving London was that Parliament had furiously refused to accept the American preliminary treaty.

In January the Preliminary Treaty with the Bourbon Alliance was signed amid much formal celebration by the participating representatives. Alan was confident that Shelburne could get it agreed by Parliament, as this treaty was proposed by the victors, not the vanquished. Tom asked what next. 'If all goes well we should have it ratified and be back home before summer' Alan assured him. 'Then I can expect to be handsomely reimbursed by the Exchequer and you can ask for the Madras governorship!' Katy had forgotten Tom's ambition to further his career with the East India Company and it made her reflect on her own views of returning to India. She realised she would find India stifling, and she did not mean just the climate, compared to Paris.

Matters then moved faster than expected. Within a month, they heard Shelburne had been forced to resign, ostensibly over Parliament's objections to the American treaty. Tom suspected it was more to do with a revolt led by members of his own Whig party, which had been noticeably brewing back in December. It meant Alan no longer represented the King's government and would have to await the outcome of Parliament's deliberations with the King. It was several weeks before there was news of a new government. It was reported that the King had been forced to accept an extraordinary combination of the Tory, Lord North, and Whig, Charles Fox, in a fourth government in less than a year, and again without a general election. Vergennes was not amused. As an embarrassed Alan said on his return from Versailles, if the French intellectuals were thinking of a Parliamentary form of government, the British example would make them think twice. Not long after, Alan learnt that a friend of Lord North, David Hartley, had been sent to renegotiate with the Americans. 'Not much hope of that. Poor fellow's just being set up as a scapegoat.' It was also confirmed that Alan was to be replaced by Lord Manchester to conclude the final treaty with the French and Spanish. 'There goes any chance of Alan's knighthood,' confided Tom to Katy.

As they made preparations for the handover, Tom began to speculate on his next position, preferably with the Company. He naturally included Katy in his plans, but she felt increasingly unsure of how she could cope with being his consort in either London or Madras. She realised how much she had grown in confidence in Tom's company and how well she had fitted in with the society that frequented the Perregaux salon. She confided in Adèle who initially took the view that the lovers should not be separated. However, she soon warmed to the alternative: Catherine could stay in Paris as originally intended. She now had friends here. She was young, very attractive and, she suggested tactfully, she had some money of her own, perhaps? That was all very well but could she bear to part with Tom, who was so much part of her new life? As the cabriolet wheeled her back, she veered between dread of losing him and excitement of making her own way in the world.

It was harrowing to see Tom's reaction to her telling him she was reluctant to follow him. 'But what will you do? Is there someone else?'

She assured him there was not and could never be. Perhaps she would be the lady-companion to Mme Fourniels. He wanted to believe her. He looked around the room they had spent so much together in, as if seeing the detail for the first time. She kept her head down, wishing this interview to end. Tom recovered his poise.

'I should have seen this coming. Sooner or later our relationship would be under strain in more conventional circumstances. I was able to forget the future while with you on the *Zeeuw* or here under Alan's patronage. We've been engaged in a fabulous production these past couple of years but, you're right. I – we, rather – must take a deep breath and face reality.' Tom could not be totally rational about the separation though. 'I will always love you, you know, Katy.'

'Oh, Tom, I'm so sorry.'

He held up a hand, staying her interruption. 'If we must part, I want to be sure you'll at least be comfortable and able to avoid falling into bad company.'

'I hope you do not include the coterie in that category!'

'No, indeed. But please allow me to arrange with M. Perregaux a small annuity for you.'

'But I have…'

'No, I insist!'

Before she could argue further he clasped her to him and smothered her protests in a lingering kiss. That night they made passionate love, as if to compensate for the lack of it in the future.

—⁂—

The next few days were hectic. Alan made arrangements with all the relevant officials and invited Lord Manchester to take over the same establishment that he had taken from Grenville. 'The cook, though, has readily agreed to join my London establishment,' Alan crowed. Alan was first to leave, having an appointment with Lord Manchester at Dover, leaving Tom and Katy to spend their last few nights together. Adèle had readily agreed to accommodate Catherine and her maid in rue du Sentier until she was ready to move on. The day before they were due to go their separate ways, there was a surprise for Katy: Tom told her that he had arranged for her portrait to be done for him by Elisabeth Vigée Le Brun. It would have to be included in her next display at the Salon, of course, but it would then be sent on to him in London.

'But that's so expensive!' she cried.

'Katy, my dearest, trust me to have learnt sufficient negotiating skills these past months to get a significant discount from that artist. She was keen to have someone as young and gorgeous as you as a sitter and she knows it will attract more business!' The following day, they made their farewells and parted with a kiss.

'Good luck, Tom.'

'*Sois sage*, Katy.' As his carriage turned out of sight, Catherine fingered her ship pendant and thought wistfully to herself: That is the last time I shall be called Katy.

Still Paris

While Vigée Le Brun enjoyed depicting Catherine as more sensuous than demur, she was careful to avoid portraying her as a voluptuous Boucher beauty. The portrait attracted a lot of attention while it was on display at the Salon and inevitably people wanted to know who this stunning young Mme Grand was. Catherine was thrilled to be the centre of so much admiration and grateful to Tom for inadvertently creating so many rivals. Tom had written to her, telling her of his new young bride. 'You would love her,' he wrote (Catherine snorted). He went on to say they were sailing to Madras in a fortnight's time (another sea romance, she chuckled), and that the recent treaty with the Mysore ruler meant they should enjoy a peaceful and prosperous time there. He concluded with saying how he missed her and had such good memories of their time in Paris. Catherine wished him every happiness and lots of children. She did not regret her decision to part.

Now she was unattached, a delighted Mme Fourniels was quick to invite her to meet her nephew, Nicolas de Lessart, the director of the *Compagnie des Indes* that had been mentioned to her before, who lived with her nearby in rue Vivienne. Nicolas was the same generation as Jean Perregaux, whom he knew well, and had been informed by his aunt of Catherine and Tom's diplomatic mission. He was pleased to hear that she was staying on in Paris and asked politely after her family in Chandernagore. Catherine admitted that she had not heard from them, which prompted him to enquire as to the married name of her sister. Remarkably it turned out that Catherine's brother-in-law, Michel de Calnois, was a cousin of Nicolas. Nicolas had not heard from him for a year but expected the peace treaty's restoration of Chandernagore to the *Compagnie des Indes* would allow their respective families to be re-established. And, he noted smiling broadly, 'That makes us cousins!'

It was a piece of luck for Catherine. Until then she had dared only accept invitations from those neighbours that Adèle could vouch for. She was surprised he was not married and wondered if he was a widower. So she had asked him why there was no Madam de Lessart and he had said he had yet to find a suitable lady. Catherine suspected he had not tried very hard and was aware his mother was a strong influence in his domestic life. Nicholas could be very serious and set in his ways. He treated her as a much younger sister to whom he could introduce the more interesting aspects of Paris life and that suited Catherine fine. He obviously found it an agreeable distraction from his work on rebuilding the fortunes of the *Compagnie des Indes*, and readily took his cousin to the various musical and stage functions. Naturally tongues would wag, but neither of them minded as it was an arrangement of mutual benefit.

That June the city was swathed in a strange and smelly haze of dust that Catherine learnt had enveloped the whole country, or so the papers said. Despite the sun being dimmed as a result, it was a scorching hot summer – as hot as Bengal, thought Catherine – so that only those whose livelihood depended on it ventured outdoors. There were any number of rumours which reminded Catherine of those scientific debates which Tom had relayed back from the cafés. Even Jean Perregaux, who called the bitter smell sulphurous, speculated that it might be to do with a volcanic eruption, a natural explosion in certain parts of the world which he had to explain to Catherine. She found it too far-fetched as an explanation but politely refrained from arguing. Rather, she concentrated on looking after Adèle who had developed a persistent hacking cough, a common complaint at present, the doctor had said and added, as an aside to Catherine, that it had proved fatal for many in the city. Consequently she did not see her cousin Nicolas, or anyone else for that matter, for several weeks. There were sudden strong storms, worse than the Indian monsoon, but more short-lived. By August the air cleared and the temperature became more bearable so that normal Paris life could resume.

Only then did Nicolas get back in touch, inviting her to accompany him on a visit to view the follies in Parc Monceau. She was pleased to do so and took some trouble over her appearance for the first time in months. After all, this was a favourite venue in which to see and be seen. Having admired the strange tributes to antiquity, they sat down overlooking the lily pond.

'I've heard from Michel de Calnois,' Nicolas opened. 'He and your sister are well and expect the English East India Company to hand over Chandernagore shortly, now that the peace treaty is concluded.'

'That is very good news.' Catherine was pleased for them. It had been some three years since they had parted and it could not have been easy for them in that time.

'So, Catherine, what are your plans?' he asked. He could readily secure her a passage back to Chandernagore if she wished?

Catherine thought about it. 'I've no wish to return to Bengal. There is nothing for me there. George, my former husband, has his own life now and I am not part of it.' It was the answer he expected.

'As you are staying in Paris, I shall be delighted to be your companion, you know.' She did indeed know and was thankful for the offer. The Perregaux were grateful for her support through the terrible summer and had made it clear she was welcome to stay on with them.

—⁂—

That autumn the table talk over dinner was all about the balloon experiments of the Montgolfier brothers. If a balloon could travel some distance in the air, could people travel with it? 'I get dizzy just going up Notre Dame,' as one of the guests said. So Nicolas took Catherine to see the latest experiment performed before the Royal Family and a sizeable crowd. The balloon had previously taken some domestic animals in a basket for a flight of a couple of miles and the animals had been retrieved unaffected by the height. So the next stage was to have a person do the same and it was going to attract a massive crowd. Nicolas was confident he could secure a decent vantage point for Catherine and his aunt and it was a wise move. The whole of Paris turned out that November day to see the two volunteer pilots doff their hats to the multitude from some 250 feet up before being wafted away over the suburbs.

'That is amazing. I could not have believed it possible. They are so brave,' exclaimed Catherine.

'We are no longer chained to the earth,' said Nicolas somewhat pompously. The crowd continued to mingle for hours later, speculating excitedly about the implications. Catherine's elation was magnified by the feeling that she too was taking off – as an independent lady.

It was indeed a good time for Catherine to be in Paris. She and Nicolas enjoyed the social whirl of new performances, talk of new scientific discoveries and the shifting politics. As an alternative to Parc Monceau, the Duc d'Orléans had rebuilt his Palais-Royale gardens into a pleasure garden surrounded by wide covered arcades, with shops and restaurants. There was even a stable with horses for hire. When Catherine confessed she had yet to ride a horse, Nicholas immediately engaged a riding instructor for her to practise there with him. As expected, gossip gathered about them and it was commonly believed Catherine was Nicolas's mistress. It could be distressing to have such slanders spread but Elisabeth Vigée Le Brun assured Catherine that she was not alone. 'Apparently I am the mistress of Colonne, the Finance minister, and that simply from painting his portrait!'

'Surely no one believes that?'

'People believe only what they want to believe. Besides, Beaumarchais has ensured they think the worst of anyone of status,' sighed the painter of aristocracy.

—⁓—

As the months went by, Catherine learned to be more thick-skinned and careful whom she spoke of to whom. Nevertheless, she was aware that Nicholas was becoming embarrassed about the gossip. It seemed he did not share his friends' view that to have a mistress was only to be expected of a man in his position. Catherine suspected his mother had hopes of a favourable match still and would prefer him to be obviously available. Whatever the reason, he was seeing less of her. There were plenty of new faces in the rue du Sentier, however. Since the conclusion of the peace treaty, Jean Perregaux was being visited by a number of his clients from England and Hanover – King George's other kingdom, Catherine was reminded – and his establishment had become a hive of activity. Of those who courted her attentions, she found the vicomte de Lambertyre the most agreeable. If he had a wife, she was looking after their children in some distant fiefdom of his. He was younger than most and his advances were considerate enough for her to recognise he was interested in more than a brief enjoyment of her favours. It was flattering. He it was who told her of the new British ambassador, the Duke of Dorset.

'And he has brought with him his mistress, Giovanna Bacelli, and their six-year-old son!' he added.

Catherine recognised the name. 'Why, I saw her dance at the King's Theatre in London. She was magnificent!'

'She still is, my dear, I assure you. She is to dance at the new Théâtre de la Porte Saint-Martin. I should be delighted if you would agree to accompany me to her performance there.'

Catherine was thrilled. She had been mesmerised by Noverre's troupe in London and never expected to be able to see such again. It would be worth the gossip to be taken there by the vicomte and if it fuelled more tittle-tattle, she was old enough at twenty-seven for it no longer to upset her.

She was not surprised, then, that she saw a lot more of the vicomte as he sought to seduce her. She certainly enjoyed his advances and made it clear that she admired him, but no more. Undeterred, he made his proposal that she should accept his patronage. Over coffee with Mme Perregaux, Mme Vigée Le Brun and Mme Sullivan, she told them of his proposal and their reaction was predictable. Adèle saw no need for her to move out and feared for her reputation: 'There will be no going back!'

Elisabeth Vigée Le Brun was more pragmatic: 'He's more of a gentleman than most and will not treat you like a possession.'

Eleanora Sullivan welcomed the move: 'Believe me, the doors it closes are those you wouldn't want to enter anyway.' It wasn't as discouraging as she had feared.

'You've changed,' said Adèle, which Catherine chose to interpret as her being more mature. Knowing each other well, the ladies were full of well-meaning advice. From their respective vantage points, they were all agreed that gentlemen rarely like to have clever women as companions. Catherine believed Tom to be an exception, but generally, she agreed, they were right. They advised her to be careful to cultivate her blond allure and be more playful rather than assertive. The advice descended into more intimate modes of behaviour and the ladies ended up giggling like naughty children.

So Catherine joined the vicomte de Lambertyre in his prestigious house on the Chaussée d'Antin. They soon settled into an amicable relationship. She was his attractive status symbol and he was her solicitous benefactor. Certainly, they enjoyed their natural appetites but affection was limited to the polite regard of an arranged marriage. Catherine discerned greater affection between Eleanora and Quintin and wondered if love grew with familiarity. Still, the vicomte remained most attentive and Catherine enjoyed keeping him amused. To be seen in his company at the Palais-Royale, on the boulevard du Temple or in the Parc Monceau caused her no concern, indeed, quite the opposite. Catherine felt there need be no shame in being on a par with her friend, Eleanora Sullivan or, indeed, Giovanna Bacelli.

Perhaps because Jacques Necker was now a neighbour in the Chaussée d'Antin, the vicomte was in a position to keep her well informed of the country's finances which, for all the personal wealth evident among their circle of friends, continued to deteriorate. Indeed, she was shocked to be told the royal treasury was declared empty that August. So that, like most people, she was delighted when Necker was reinstated as Finance Minister. And, not least, because her cousin Nicolas was appointed by him to be one of the three commissaries who were to investigate the Ministry's past conduct.

Beyond the confines of their comfortable house, though, the gaiety of Paris life was replaced by a more sombre mood. Necker's appointment coincided with a particularly ruinous summer as a result of a freak storm that devastated crops across the whole country. To make matters worse, there followed the longest, most severe winter in living memory. Normal public activity ceased as Parisians kept indoors, huddled over their fires. The price of bread was reported to have doubled and was still rising. It was not a time to be poor and Catherine took great care to be the indispensable mistress of the vicomte's household. With the advent of spring, the focus returned to national politics. Vicomte de Lambertyre was one of those aristocrats who joined the First Estate and then the newly formed National Assembly determined to do away with the old and create some new form of governance. He had mentioned to her his hope for a form of constitutional monarchy, not dissimilar to that in Britain, and Catherine knew his views to be the same as, if not formed by, the views of a neighbour, the Count de Mirabeau.

Week after week the vicomte returned home from Versailles exhausted by the National Assembly's endless parleys, discussions that struck Catherine as tedious, however vehemently the various parties discussed decrees and manoeuvred the monarchy. Still, she was well aware that the whole of Paris was in a state of excitement, expecting a long-overdue release from the strictures of the present archaic establishment. When she heard of Necker's disgrace and departure, she was as angry as the next Parisian about it but was cautious enough not to join the furious demonstrations gathering to the south-east. From the upper windows she could hear the tocsin being called, the drums, and the sound of a mob set on plunder, which continued on and off throughout the next couple of days. Catherine recalled what she'd been told of the Gordon riots. It had been weeks before the military had restored order in that London rampage and she hoped it would not take as long for the same to be concluded here in Paris. So she anxiously waited for her vicomte to return from Versailles while the nearby tumult reached a crescendo. The following day was relatively calm when he got back.

'I thought I heard cannon yesterday,' she said, 'has the army restored peace?'

He was surprisingly jubilant as he told her that the cannon she heard was to do with the attack on, and fall of, the Bastille prison and how the King had agreed to withdraw the troops from around Paris. This, he said, marked the end of the King's authority and thus freedom for the National Assembly to draw up a new constitution. Catherine's surprise was quickly replaced by relief at his confidence.

—⁂—

Over the following months, there was a succession of dramatic announcements: individual liberty was enshrined in a declaration of rights, representative institutions were set up and civil and fiscal equality expressed. A National Guard was formed early on, soon followed by the abolition of the old feudal provinces, municipalities, nobility and titles. De Lambertyre was one of many who immediately dropped the aristocratic prefix of 'de', while others incorporated it into their surname. Catherine could not fail to be aware of the violence that accompanied these changes, whether bread riots in the provinces or the forced removal of the Royal Family from Versailles to Paris. Lambertyre told her it was the only way to get the King to agree to the Constitution. Months passed as he continued to work on the new proposals of the National Assembly, while Catherine took note of the mood of the city, positive in its support for the Assembly. Her confidence gradually returned as Lambertyre reported on Mirabeau's remarkable construction of a new constitutional monarchy. On the anniversary of the fall of the Bastille, she joined Lambertyre in the massive *Fête de la Fédération* celebration on the Champ de Mars. The whole of Paris must have attended, the crowd swelled by the representatives from the eighty-three new *départements*. Listening to the solemn oath taken by the commander of the National Guard, the President of the Assembly and King Louis XVI, Catherine believed at that moment, as did the rest of those present, in the sincerity of the King and the affection for him of his subjects. She was not the only one to find the whole well-organised event awe-inspiring. There followed balls, sports and illuminations. It was a magical time and Catherine felt proud and delighted to have been a part of it.

Flight

Sadly it was not to last. It seemed symbolic when Mirabeau, their neighbour as much as the President of the Assembly, died the following April. Monsieur Lambertyre, as he was now addressed, told her how much the Assembly was increasingly riven with discord as Republicans challenged the Monarchists and the King vacillated between cooperation and betrayal. However he could not satisfy her curiosity as to how stable the government was. Eleanora was, if anything, more pessimistic. She told Catherine that Quintin was set on relocating to London. The Duke of Dorset had not returned from leave back in England and had been replaced as ambassador by a young English lord who was clearly out of his depth trying to make sense of a disintegrating court. When asked, his advice to the British residents was to leave Paris. Eleanora and Quintin loved Paris but felt it was time for them to join Quintin's Scottish relatives in London. Catherine was welcome to come with them if she wished.

Catherine felt the British were overreacting. She had no intention of leaving Paris and, besides, she had no connection with England. She thanked Eleanora for her kind offer and wished her friend a fond adieu. Nevertheless, Catherine needed some reassurance and so visited her cousin Monsieur Delessart as he now was, who, after a brief spell as Finance Minister was now Minister of the Interior. Nicolas looked the part in his elegant attire though somewhat older without the powdered wig that was now unfashionable. However harassed he was, he retained that old-world politeness she was used to from him. He was, as always, pleased to see her and commented on her good fortune in being the protégée of a wealthy member of the Assembly in these vicissitudes of fortune. She learnt something of how difficult it was for him to be an effective minister when effectively subordinate to the key members of the Assembly, but little else. She left him no more reassured than when she had arrived.

As the months went by, Catherine's unease grew. She was saddened more than alarmed to hear that the new Le Brun property in nearby rue du Gros Chenet had been vandalised, such was the growing unrest targeted at the better known but less protected recipients of royalist patronage. It was no surprise to then hear that Elisabeth Vigée Le Brun had left Paris, together with her daughter and governess, by public coach for Italy. Nor was she the only one. Ex-vicomte de Lambertyre confirmed that a number of aristocratic members of the Assembly had decided to slip away and await events from outside France. He himself was concerned that the general unwillingness to pay for anything, let alone taxes or rents, had reduced his own disposable income. Catherine became increasingly concerned and she begged him to take precautions for their safety. He reassured her that, as a member of the Assembly, he was more secure than some of the former nobility he knew. Nevertheless he was prepared to hire a young Swiss soldier to guard their house for Catherine's peace of mind. Catherine was glad of his support and silently pleased she had not become too independent.

Catherine could not help but be aware that the political situation was deteriorating. The fragmentation of the Assembly into different factions continued and elections were held for a replacement, more tightly controlled, Legislative Assembly. Monsieur Lambertyre did not stand for that election and when the National Assembly was dissolved at the end of September to the satisfaction of the Parisians, he talked rather to Catherine of the nobles he knew who had slipped across the Rhine to join the German princes. He referred to them as 'émigrés', those who had left the country in disagreement with the way the country was now governed, though their different expectations made them a pretty disparate group.

Catherine was now worried for the future and paid another evening visit to cousin Nicolas, recently appointed Foreign Minister. It was remarkable how quickly he changed portfolios and Catherine knew that to ask the reason was to encourage a lengthy explanation that would be lost on her. Besides, her interest was more for the present than the past. Over dinner Nicolas confirmed a lot of what she had read in the newspapers; that, despite the Rhenish princes disbanding the émigré forces, the Austrians, whose Belgium territory was only a hundred miles from Paris, threatened to support the émigrés against the French government by force. He thought war with Austria was a real possibility as both the Assembly and the King, albeit for different reasons, were eager to provoke it.

'But you don't, do you?' she asked.

'Of course not,' he replied. 'While it would be foolhardy for me to challenge the Assembly, I'm doing my best to get the more sympathetic nations to bring pressure to bear on the Austrians.' This was an aspect of diplomacy new to Catherine.

'Can – or will – they help?' she wondered out loud. Nicolas said he could only hope. Britain and Prussia's neutrality would be a good second best. He was sending the Bishop of Autun to London as Britain would want to avoid disruption to its trade through Flanders. 'The same bishop who officiated at the Fête?' she asked, surprised a civil cleric should be entrusted with such a task.

Nicolas corrected himself. 'He's the elected administrator for the *département* of Paris now. More to the point, Talleyrand is more fluent and intelligent than most of the Assembly members that I can rely on!' He advised her to stay the night rather than venture the distance back to the Chaussée d'Antin in the Faubourg Montmartre. She assumed he did not mean to share her bed and in that she was not mistaken. It was a welcome change not to be thought of as purely an object of desire.

Catherine slept well there and came late to breakfast to find Nicolas already closeted on ministry affairs. He had left her a document. The covering note explained this was a passport should she need it. Catherine penned her thanks to him before leaving for the Chaussée d'Antin. A surprise awaited her there. Her maid was relieved to see her and told her that the vicomte had left in his coach and some of the other staff were missing too. Lambertyre had left her a note – everyone was leaving her notes today, she observed. In it, he explained he had gone to visit his friends across the Rhine and would return soon. What did he mean by 'soon', she thought? Looking around she was reassured that he had taken nothing of value with him. It had all the evidence of a decision taken in haste and she worried what had driven him to leave her at such short notice and with so little explanation. It was pointless speculating. Her maid, the cook and the young soldier were still here and could not enlighten her.

So she quickly reassured them, 'Please understand, I am staying here and I'd like you to also. You will continue to be paid, though by me if necessary.' They nodded acceptance and Catherine suspected if they had any alternative they would have exercised it along with the rest of the staff. She wrote another note that morning and told her maid to deliver it to Jean Perregaux in rue du Sentier. Fortunately the new paper money, assignats, could be supplied by him to her without attracting the same attention as a bag of coin. It should last until the vicomte's return.

As the days extended to weeks without news from the vicomte, Catherine considered her position. Although yet again abandoned by her partner, she had wondered if she would have gone with him if he had asked. Her friends were in Paris; his were across the Rhine. She suspected he had left her here to ensure his property was not confiscated as the Assembly had frequently threatened of émigrés. She liked to think she was holding it all in trust for him. Food was plentiful, thanks to the new Paris authorities, the same new authority that had renamed her street 'rue de Mirabeau'. She could do worse than stay in this relatively secure suburb and await events.

And events moved rapidly. Tensions mounted when news broke of a pact between Austria and Prussia and Catherine was shocked to hear that Nicolas Delessart had been arrested for treason and a new Foreign Minister had been appointed in his place. She learnt that her cousin had been taken to Orléans for trial and realised there was nothing she could do but comfort his aunt as best she could. Mme Fourniels was indeed distraught. She had been delighted with his promotion to high rank and he had clearly given her no indication of how fragile his various ministerial positions really were. Catherine shared her concern and hoped whatever charges would be levelled at him could be soon disproved and his return to Paris assured. Not that his successor did any better: within weeks, France was at war with Austria. Recalling her last conversation with Nicolas, Catherine felt it unrealistic to join in the popular mood of defiance and conviction. Sure enough, that national elation soon turned to fury as news of the desertions and defeats in Flanders arrived in the capital. Recriminations and accusations abounded. When foreigners in Paris were put under surveillance that May, Catherine, still officially Mrs Grand, made a point of being as French as her surroundings and escaped the authorities' attention. Then the Austrian forces crossed the border from Belgium and its commander issued a threatening proclamation vowing to free the French King. It did not help at all. Groups of armed *fédérés* from the provinces started to arrive in the capital, processing round the poorer neighbourhoods with drums and songs, audible to the higher Montmartre residents.

Catherine again heard the tocsin peal across Paris that fateful August morning and realised that there was to be a repeat of the June attack on the Royal Family in the Tuileries. Now, as then, Catherine was determined to keep indoors and await the outcome, but her cook was more curious and slipped out to join the massing crowds. Catherine went upstairs where she felt safer despite the heat of the day. From there she could hear the undulating din of the mob in the distance. She thought she heard rifle fire but it did not last whereas the crowd's clamour continued. It all seemed to be happening in a Paris she did not recognise. Her thoughts were disturbed by the sudden appearance of her maid at her chamber threshold.

'Madam, I'm frightened. I'm told there is a group of the commune's *fédérés* approaching from Place Vendome and that they mean business.'

'Who told you? And what sort of business? Speak!'
Catherine went across to the window in time to see a red-capped
mob just turning into their rue de Mirabeau, which had become
otherwise empty of any man or beast. Seeing her Swiss Guard
at the door the group broke into a cheer and ran towards him.
Catherine yelled to him to come inside but he took one look
down the street and made off in the opposite direction chased
by the howling rabble. Catherine watched horrified as he fell to
their pikes and hatchets, before they moved on to search out
their next victim.

The street was empty as Catherine approached the gruesome
body of the young man she had barely known. She had seen a
dead body or two in Bengal, but those had died from natural
causes and never been so mutilated. Numbed, she arranged
his limbs in a more dignified manner, tried to stammer out a
mixture of compassion and prayer, but couldn't think what else
to do and returned to her house to wash the blood from her
hands and reflect on the implications of such a pointless murder.
But her mind was numb and she could make no sense of it. It
was the cook who nervously explained on her return from the
city centre that there had been an insurrection and how the
King was taken and the Swiss Guard had all been murdered
by the mob for putting up some resistance. She had seen their
naked bodies piled up on the side of the courtyard there. In her
opinion, their house guard's only crime was to have shared the
same uniform. Everywhere she went, she had seen businesses
shuttered and barred, and that the normal sights and sounds of
the City were eerily absent. She had worse news for Catherine:

'They say the prisoners who were being brought from
Orléans to face trial here in Paris stopped at Versailles this
morning, madam. They say most of them were then taken to

one side and executed. Just like that. No warning; no reason. Just killed. They say, madam, that one of those killed was the ex-minister Delessart.'

Catherine reached for the nearest chair, stunned. Could this really be true? After what she had just witnessed, it could well be. The cook could add nothing further and retreated to the back of the house. Catherine had to put aside the horror and think hard of her predicament. She held out her hands until they stopped trembling. She ran through the options as she saw them and summoned her maid and the cook, the only staff left.

'I shall be going to rue du Sentier for a while. Please keep the house secure until I return.'

They nodded, keeping their thoughts to themselves. Reminded of Lambertyre's note, she did not add 'soon'. It would be a lie. She went back upstairs and hurriedly pack a few essentials in a portmanteau. She left the house without a backward glance.

She had no intention of staying in Paris and made for the terminus for the public coaches northwards, keeping as much as possible to the quieter streets. It was past five in the afternoon when normally Parisians would have finished work and be making their way to their favourite cafés or shops. Now there were few people about and the empty streets echoed to their urgent footsteps, which only heightened Catherine's sense of dread. In contrast, the coach terminal was a mass of seething humanity, pushing and shoving with bags in one hand and waving assignats with the other. It seemed impossible. Putting on her best Fanny accent, Catherine said loudly, 'If you please, I'm English. *Je suis anglaise.* Make way, please, I need to get home to England.' A few faces turned curiously towards her but she got no nearer to the Inn yard. 'So are we,' said a voice behind her. She turned to find a lady on the arm of an elderly gentleman. 'It's hopeless. And there's not a post-chaise to be had,' the man said. 'We're thinking of hiring a private coach. Would you care to join us if we can find one?' Catherine was effusive with her thanks and they exchanged introductions. Mrs Grand, then, breathed a sigh of relief and offered to take them to where she believed a private coach might be had. There was more safety in numbers, and he was prepared to carry her portmanteau for her. They barely kept up with her as she strode off, the clammy heat of the day emphasising the almost palpable tension in the streets.

At first the staff refused them entry, but a distressed Mme Fourniels recognised Catherine and let them in. Of course she had heard of her nephew Nicolas's murder and Catherine spent some time trying to console her. Once she felt the elderly lady was up to it, she begged her help in having the Delessart coachman take them part of, if not all, the way to the coast. Mme Fourniels had always been a true friend to Catherine and she did not let her down now. No, she herself would stay in Paris and arrange her nephew's affairs. But, yes, by all means take the English family – Catherine had forgotten their names – along too. In keeping with citizen Delassart's standing, his coach had long been made suitably anonymous. Catherine confirmed they all had passports, silently thanking her cousin Nicolas for his foresight. The English couple listened to these rapid exchanges in French and wisely didn't interrupt. Mme Fourniels asked that Catherine say goodbye before they left and Catherine went off to the carriage house to the rear of the property, trailed by the English couple. Catherine was tall for her age, but the coachman was taller. Looking down at the girl in front of him, he expressed reluctance to take to the roads and 'with the master dead, who would pay for it?' Catherine produced some assignats but he refused them and turned his back on her. *Mon Dieu*, send me strength, prayed a frustrated Catherine. Was there no end to this nightmare?

At that point the Englishman pulled Catherine aside and whispered to her that he had coin, gold coin. Without pausing to thank him, Catherine at once entered into a heated negotiation with the coachman.

'And what about the overnight stays?'

'That depends.'

And so it went on until a deal was reached. She told the Englishman the outcome, adding a tip for Delessart's ostler. As the coach and horses were being prepared, Catherine went back to say farewell to Mme Fourniels. It was an emotional leave-taking, all the more so on Catherine's part as she felt guilty that she had earlier intended to leave Paris without a goodbye to the only friend left there.

It was a much-subdued threesome who sat well back in the coach as it made its way through the outlying villages in the dying light of that warm August evening. 'Are you really English?' asked the lady. Catherine was too tired to reply and the gentleman said, 'It doesn't matter. We're much indebted to you, madam. Indeed, I suspect your assignats won't be accepted at Calais. Allow me, please, to pay at least for your passage to Dover. It is the least I can do.' Catherine, who hadn't thought beyond getting out of Paris, thanked him in turn and was soon fast asleep despite the odd jolt of the coach over the well-worn route north.

Dover

It was drizzling at Dover. It had been the same when Catherine was here ten years previously. Back then she was exuberant at going to France; now she was dejected at leaving it in such circumstances. And this time, apart from what one would expect of any busy port and shipbuilding yard, Dover was full of French émigrés, tradesmen anxious to relieve them of their financial burdens and officials determined to be, well, officious. The hostelries were full and the coaches fully booked. Tired, hungry, cold and damp, Catherine needed to find a quiet spot. She toiled up towards the castle and sat on a low wall looking over the gently undulating grey sea towards a France in bloody turmoil. The tears rolled down her cheeks as she sobbed in self-pity. Getting more chilled by the minute and having cried enough, she dabbed her eyes, sat up a little straighter and said to herself, 'I'll show them, I'll show them all!'

'Well, what have we here?' a voice behind her interrupted her thoughts. She turned to find a young man with a dog on a lead. He was dressed for the weather, a long dark coat, a tricorn hat and stout footwear. He made an extravagant bow, as best the dog would allow, and introduced himself. 'Lieutenant Belcher, ma'am. Forgive me for saying so, but you look in need of some assistance?' Catherine couldn't help but smile as his dog pulled him off balance and he fell in a heap beside her, his hat tumbling off to reveal a strong-jawed, more weathered face than most that she had come across.

'I rather think it is you who needs assistance,' she replied, retrieving his hat. 'I'm Mrs Grand.' She stood up and better arranged her clothes while she appraised him. 'I confess I am in need of somewhere to stay temporarily, if you know of somewhere not already taken.'

'Well, Mrs Grand,' he said, now clearly unsure of her nationality, 'permit me to escort you to somewhere suitable, if you don't mind a detour while I return this hound to its rightful owner.'

Catherine found the conversation most agreeable as they walked back down to the port and up the other side. Nat, as he asked to be called, had a great deal of charm and Catherine suspected it was not the first time he had accosted young ladies fresh off the packet boat. Far from minding, she saw the advantages of the situation. Mindful of the events of her last day in Paris, she thought there were worse things than being picked up by a confident young gentleman.

Having returned the hound to a grateful whiskered old gentleman whose wooden leg explained the loan of the dog, he escorted her away from the noise of the busy port. Catherine was reassured by his being greeted on the way, she noticed, by a number of elegantly dressed locals. He halted in a street of smart new terraced houses, which stood in stark contrast to the nearby overgrown ruins of an old priory.

'Welcome to my humble abode,' he said as he ushered her in.

He took off his hat and coat and bade her sit down at the table in the front room while he addressed someone to the rear of the house: 'A couple of hot toddies, please, Ed.' Ed was clearly a retainer rather than a relative and didn't stay longer than to serve up their drinks and some bread, ham and cheese. 'So,' Nat asked jovially, 'are you really married to an Englishman?' To which she countered, 'Are you really a Lieutenant?' They understood each other.

'Come, you need to take off those wet clothes or you'll catch your death of cold. I've some dry stuff upstairs.' Catherine allowed him to take her upstairs and show her into a bedroom. The room was as well-furnished as the rest of the house that she had seen but with nothing that gave a clue to his occupation. He laid a fire while she picked out a shirt and breeches. 'Good choice,' he said as he left the room. Catherine turned her back on the door as she undid her bodice and couldn't help hearing him tiptoe back in behind her. He put one arm round her waist and the other lifted her hair to plant a kiss on the side of her neck. 'You really are ravishing,' he murmured. She turned in his arm and started to unbutton his waistcoat. She had missed this long enough.

Later, dressed in her own dried clothes and downstairs, she confided to him that she was married but her husband was in India. 'Ah, a Company man. Not a ship's captain, by any chance?' he asked.

'No, but he transferred from the military because the pay was barely enough to make ends meet,' said Catherine as she fingered the silver cutlery and fine porcelain.

'Quite right, it isn't. But I *was* briefly a lieutenant in the Buffs.'

'And now?'

'Now I'm a wholesaler,' he said enigmatically and went on to ask how she had come to be alone in Dover.

Catherine tucked some stray hair behind her ear and explained how she had had to leave Paris in a hurry in the midst of a riot, having had her concierge murdered on her own doorstep. She admitted she was at a loss as to what to do as she had left all her jewellery and other valuables behind.

'If they are still there, I could go and fetch them for you,' he suggested gallantly.

'Seriously?'

'Why not? I'm at a loose end – between ships, so to speak – and it would be relatively easy for me since we are at peace with France for a change. You could then reimburse me for the expense.'

It was such an unexpected offer that Catherine was wary. 'Really? We hardly know each other.'

'Oh, I think I do,' he said, placing his hand at the source of all her excitement upstairs.

Her hand reached for his equivalent sensitive spot and softly said, 'I believe I could make it worth your while.'

It was the following day that they discussed the realities of the adventure. She confirmed that she really was English so that the contents of the house should not have been impounded and drew up a long list of the precious jewellery, coin, and plate valuables in Lambertyre's house.

'Phew,' he said, 'that is more than I expected. It's a heavy cartload. I'll need help,' and he mentioned a friend, O'Dryer, who'd happily accompany him. 'We will need passports and a power of attorney to prove our right to take it, of course. It'll be a change to handle clean merchandise,' he added with a grin.

Seeing her concern, he explained himself carefully: 'As you know, the captains of Company ships are allowed a certain amount of private trade: it gives them an incentive to bring home the cargo safely.' She nodded. 'Well, for those bound for London, whether from the East or the West Indies, I can give them a good price if they drop certain of their personal cargo off with us en route and I then sell it at a reasonable margin. That's what I mean about being in the wholesale business.'

Catherine began to understand. 'Let me guess, Nat, your price will reflect the absence of excise duty.'

'You catch on fast, love. I have plenty of willing customers in London and thereabouts. It also means that with those customers, I'll be able to turn your valuables into cash without you having to pay a sale room's commission!' he added with a flourish. Catherine felt more confident about trusting him to deliver the treasure trove to her.

So Nat made his arrangements. While he was away, she was welcome to stay here as his guest and let Ed deal with his customers, and provide the food, drink and fuel from those tradesmen with whom he had plenty of credit. In due course all was prepared and it was time to say adieu.

'If I'm not back before the Hunter's Moon, here is the address of a friend of mine in London. He may not be much use, but he does have good connections,' he told her. Catherine looked at the name and address.

'J.P.?'

'Yes he's a magistrate.'

'But your business is not legal, surely.'

He winked as he told her, 'Magistrates deal with criminals, not wholesalers. Trust me,' he added as he left.

'I do. Oh I really do,' she added a silent prayer.

The weeks passed and to occupy her time, Catherine got into a routine of walking the old man's dog.

'You one of them émigrés?' he had asked her and Catherine had not known how to answer.

'I'm from India,' she said eventually.

'Ah, right then,' he said, giving it an emphasis as if it explained everything. 'I'm sorry for those refugees,' he said, pointing with his clay pipe at the harbour. 'Mind you, if they were more like us, they'd not be in the mess they're in,' he confided confidently.

That, thought Catherine, thinking of Lambertyre's long discussions with Mirabeau, is the sum of the case for a constitutional monarchy!

Being out with the dog, she'd soon got to know, and be known by, Nat's acquaintances. She'd found Dover was the first to get reliable news from the Continent. Thus she heard about the September massacres, many times over, and the victory of the Republic, as it now styled itself, at Valmy. But still no news of Nat. The nights were particularly difficult.

There were times she woke up terrified just before the *fédéré* succeeded in impaling her on his pike. Then the familiar bedroom furniture took shape in the moonlight and she knew it for the recurrent nightmare it had been. Gradually, the night-time fear receded but the daytime frustration remained. By the end of October, she began to fear that Nat's honest task for her had proved more dangerous than his normal contraband business. Philip Francis had not replied to her letter addressed to him at the House of Commons. She had even written to Alan Fitzherbert care of his London club, but its secretary had replied informing her that Lord St Helens, as he now was, was currently

His Majesty's ambassador in Madrid. She was pleased for him but could think of no one else to contact. Then she remembered the address that Nat had left her and penned a brief letter introducing herself to Mr William Wickham J.P. He replied suggesting a date for her to meet him in London. She would have to borrow the coach fare from Ed.

The coach went no further than an Inn on the south side of London Bridge, which left her struggling through that congested entrance to the City. The grey eddies of the river Thames matched the grey of the threatening clouds overhead. Catherine pulled her cloak closer round her as she followed the coachman's instructions towards Holborn, better paved, he assured her, than the route along The Strand. She eventually found Crown Street running south from Oxford Street and Mr Wickham's offices. She was shown into a depressingly plain room with files piled on a sideboard behind a large double pedestal desk. Mr Wickham half rose out of his chair to greet her and motioned her to one of the chairs facing him. He sat back as she explained how a friend of hers, Lt. Belcher, had not returned from a trip to France within the expected time and how he had mentioned she should contact Mr Wickham in that eventuality.

'From your accent, you're not English are you, Mrs Grand? I only ask because we are obliged to keep a register of all aliens,' he said, pointing to a bulging loose-leaf folder on his desk. This magistrate seems more interested in émigrés than criminals, she thought. She told him her English husband was still in the Company's employ in India.

'I would not worry about Lt. Belcher, madam. I had a despatch from him only yesterday.' Catherine's surprise showed. 'Please understand, he is delivering things for me in Paris. Confidential things, which is why he would not have told you.'

'Well he could have told me he was safe after all these weeks!'

'He's a cautious operator, as I think you know,' said Mr Wickham alluding no doubt to Nat's usual business. 'Rest assured he should be back in Dover in a week or two.' Wickham looked over her shoulder at the bracket clock behind her and stood up. He was about to dismiss her but his hand stopped in mid-air.

'Mrs Grand, would you know of any of the French community here in England?' Catherine was about to deny it but was intrigued enough to hazard a guess.

'Are the Perregaux here?' she ventured.

He quickly sat down again and leant forward 'You know the Perregaux?' She clearly deserved more respect. 'He was arrested in Paris early this month.' Catherine stifled a gasp. Mr Wickham raised his hand, rubbing thumb and forefinger together. 'But secured his release and is now with my brother-in-law in Lausanne.' Catherine was relieved for them and also quite surprised at the width of Mr Wickham's network.

'Would you care for a cup of tea?' he said, ringing a little bell to have refreshments brought.

Mr Wickham was interested in her Paris connections and Catherine was careful to omit any reference to her more intimate ones. He picked up on her mention of Mme Sullivan. 'Ah, yes. A remarkable woman, I'm told she did her best to smuggle the Royal Family out of Paris.' Catherine looked at his Aliens file.

'Is she here then?' she asked.

'She's not in that file. Mrs Sullivan is as officially British as you are, Mrs Grand,' he reminded her. 'However I do happen to know where she and Quintin Crauford live, if that is of use to you?'

Catherine said she would be pleased to be reacquainted with Eleanora Sullivan and he copied out the address for her.

Catherine felt more confident and took a cabriolet, or cab as they called it here, back to the Southwark coaching inn. As she settled back in the Dover coach, she pondered what service Lt. Belcher did for Mr Wickham and suspected it was more sinister than merely supplying him with occasional contraband. But at least she could expect Nat safely back soon. She also wondered about Quintin and Eleanora. They had obviously been more involved in Paris politics than she realised. She always thought Quintin Crauford was a retired gentleman of means, more interested in the arts than public affairs. It seemed that her friends was more complicated than she had thought. For the moment, though, she needed Nat to return with her valuables before she could re-establish contact with Eleanora.

Sure enough, one damp November afternoon in Dover, she saw a familiar figure mount the steps to the door. Nat took off his hat and coat, wet from the rain, much as she'd first met him. It was her turn to ask Ed for a hot toddy and, after a generous long hug, have him rest awhile before telling her his tale. He immediately assured her with pride that her cartload of treasure was now safely stowed in one of his secure caverns in the cliff. He and his friend, O'Dryer, had had quite an adventure dealing with officials who queried their passports at every checkpoint and the Paris authorities who argued his right to the contents of the house as they claimed it was the legally confiscated property of an émigré (well, Lambertyre certainly would not expect to retrieve it then, thought Catherine). Luckily they accepted Mrs Grand was English and not on that émigré list and, in the end, they had let his British obstinacy win the day – or weeks as it transpired.

Catherine enjoyed listening to his embroidered tale before sweetly adding, 'And Mr Wickham will be paying your expenses, then?'

'Ah, you've met him then.' Nat smiled. 'Perhaps half? There's O'Dryer's expenses too.'

Catherine had come to love this sort of bargaining. Besides, she was delighted and impressed with the success of his adventure. They soon went upstairs to celebrate in the same way as on that first meeting.

—⁓—

It was a busy time as Nat caught up with his business dealings and arranged for her booty to be included bit by bit in his London-bound wagon for certain of his clients. Catherine repaid her debts and opened an account with one of the two banking houses in Dover, to the amusement of Nat who preferred more tangible deposits. He rarely discussed his business with her but voiced his concern when they heard that the Republic's army had not only overrun Austrian Belgium but had crossed into the Southern Netherlands. 'But you've no trade there, have you?' queried Catherine. Nat had not. But he was aware that the French liberating the Scheldt estuary was contrary to an important Anglo-Dutch agreement, an act of aggression that could provoke Britain to join in the war on France. Already the Kent militia had been mobilised. War would be a major threat to his business.

Not that there was much business that winter. December brought more gales than usual and only needy fishermen ventured into the choppy Channel. Nat's cosy home was a convenient shelter for them both through the inclement season. However, now that she had money at her disposal, Catherine's New Year's resolution was to re-establish herself as an independent lady of means. The new year heralded calmer waters and a resumption of trade and news from France. That news continued to shock. The trial of King Louis XVI ended with his execution and, in an apparent fit of euphoria, the Republic then declared war on England and the Netherlands. War might have come sooner than Nat had expected but he had already considered his options and mentioned it might be better for him to buy back his commission. 'We're survivors, you and me, love,' he had declared with confidence. Indeed, thought Catherine, as she contemplated leaving her patron rather than being left by him as had been the case too often in the past. She had the means but she needed to be sure of the next step.

She wrote to Eleanora Sullivan explaining her interest in taking a lease on a London property and asking for her help in finding something suitable. As she had hoped, she received an open invitation to stay with Eleanor (as she now referred to herself) in the meantime since Quintin Crauford had been sent to the Netherlands on government business. As Catherine expected, Nat was quite understanding about her wish to join the expatriate community in London. They had both enjoyed a profitable relationship in many ways and were pragmatic enough to realise it was time for her to move on. Catherine instructed her Dover banker to transfer her account to Wrights bank in Covent Garden, as recommended by Eleanor, and took the London coach in far better mood than when she had last made that journey.

A cab deposited Catherine at the Crauford house in Hanover Square. She was shown into a hall full of Indian and European artefacts but dominated by a portrait of Eleanor. So that, when greeted by her, Catherine's first impression was how she had aged. And then was struck by a fearful thought that perhaps she herself had too. But there was no lack of warmth in the greeting as she was ushered into the drawing room. Eleanor confirmed the portrait was by Vigée Le Brun. 'She's now in Vienna, living off her portraits. Would you believe it, her husband got a republican divorce to protect his Paris property from confiscation!' Catherine was more impressed that Vigée Le Brun could manage independently than shocked by her husband's selfish action. Over the coming days, they exchanged stories of their escapades the previous year before addressing the important question of Catherine's future. She welcomed Eleanor's advice.

'Depends on what you can afford, of course. If you wish to join the émigré society, I would suggest lodgings in the Soho or Marylebone districts. If you're looking to attract a wealthier patron, then you need to be further out. The nearest thing to a Paris salon is Holland House on the outskirts of Kensington. The reactionary royalists are attracted to that Whig Party base. On the other hand, Mme de Stael has re-established her own constitutional monarchy salon at Juniper Court, but that's out in Surrey. It depends what you're after.'

Catherine was less sure of her welcome to, or even her interest in, London's émigré society. 'I'm not sure what I want. I don't know where I belong – London or Paris? India even!'

'But that's nonsense! Look at me: I was Italian, had an Irish husband, have a Scottish partner and recently acquired a French son-in-law!'

'I'm not looking for a patron just yet,' admitted Catherine, 'and I'm not sure anyone suitable would look twice at me.'

'Don't you believe it,' said Eleanor confidently. 'You're, what, thirty years old, and still looking a lot younger. Honestly, I'm not sure I want you still here when Quintin gets back,' she joked.

'You love him, don't you?'

'Oh, yes, Quintin is very special to me. He may not have weathered his fifty years as well as others but what I like about him is his beautiful mind and manners. He is what I think a Renaissance nobleman would have been, with wide cultivated interests. We get on well and I have the respect of the rest of the Crauford clan. Yes, I am more in love now than I ever was in my youth.'

Catherine admitted to being a bit envious. 'I don't think I'll ever fall in love again. I'm not the naïve young girl from Bengal anymore.'

'I doubt you ever were. Look, you want the security that you think only money can bring. I think you can still have the security that a considerate patron can bring.' As Catherine shook her head, Eleanor added, 'But we will have you set up properly in London first.'

———※———

Having appraised – and been appraised by – Mr Wright, her new banker, to their mutual satisfaction, Catherine spent these early spring days reacquainting herself with London. It was a very different, and much larger, London than the one she'd left a decade ago. Then, the capital was still under the shadow of the anti-papist riots; now, she saw French priests being treated sympathetically. Then, Londoners had appeared weary of waging war against the rest of the world; now, joining a war as part of a European coalition was greeted with excitement. Overall, Catherine got the impression of a more confident and tolerant London than before. There were worse places, she well knew, in which to be an expatriate. She took a lease of a house in Kensington Square, a respectable backwater, affordable now that the king was no longer at Kensington Palace. She then hired a grateful Belgium domestic, Marie, from among the refugees in Somers Town. Although she felt she could now look forward to again becoming a secure and independent member of society, there was that nagging feeling that it might last no longer than her last attempt.

London again

'Excuse me, sir, but I hailed him first!' Before reaching her, the cab had pulled up in response to the outstretched hand of a man leaning heavily on his cane several feet away. The gentleman, for so he was dressed, turned towards her and with a bow apologised in a familiar accent. An émigré, evidently. She explained in French that she had an appointment in Covent Garden. He was indeed French and explained that he too had an appointment, in his case at Lansdowne House. Perhaps they could share the cab? Catherine softened once she realised his cane was a practical aid and not merely an embellishment. When he introduced himself as Charles Talleyrand, she immediately recognised him as the ex-bishop who had been employed by her cousin Nicolas as a diplomat on behalf of Revolutionary France, and that he was younger than she had imagined despite the slight stoop over his shorter leg. They settled back in the cab, Catherine conscious he was giving her that same appraising look that she had become used to.

'I believe, monseigneur, that you knew my cousin Nicolas de Lessart?'

'Charles, please. I'm no longer a bishop,' he said automatically.

Then turning to her with genuine interest. 'So you are cousin to Nicolas. I am so sorry. He was a good, honest man.'

'I know. He did not want this war. It is why he was murdered.'

She deliberately did not say 'executed' and he commented, 'It was a brutal time.'

That was too neutral for Catherine. 'It was the worst day of my life,' she said with feeling.

'I'm so sorry,' he repeated.

Catherine probed, 'Can I ask why you are here in London?'

There was a hint of a smile as he answered, 'Because I have no wish to be rewarded for my diplomatic efforts in the same way.'

They conversed politely about lesser matters on the way along Knightsbridge, and Catherine learned that he too was a resident of Kensington Square. Before she arrived at Henrietta Street, he had her permission to call on her there. She was not only charmed by his courtly manner but also attracted by his reputation.

For the moment, though, Catherine set about managing her finances. Thomas Wright (for it was he with whom she had an appointment) provided useful advice and Catherine had learnt enough from Jean Perregaux to better judge the investments offered. She left his premises with confidence, walking briskly away from the bustle of Covent Garden, crossing Soho to the relative calm of Hanover Square. Eleanor bade her welcome and happily reintroduced her to Quintin Crauford, fresh back from the Low Countries. He looked well and was keen to tell her the latest news of the war as witnessed by his many nephews who were spread among the coalition forces gradually advancing through Belgium and the Rhineland. Catherine was content to listen to the exploits of the Crauford clan but did not regret it when he made his excuses and left her to talk with Eleanor.

Naturally, Eleanor knew of Monseigneur Talleyrand, and was eloquent in her opinion of him. Far from being an émigré at odds with the Republican government, he had arrived in England as a representative of that government before war had been declared and had been disowned by them since. Consequently he had enemies both sides of the Channel. Eleanor believed his reputation with certain ladies of standing was well founded. He was known to have a soft spot for pretty young ladies who were not afraid to speak their mind. She continued confidentially, 'I'm told that Mme de Staël, the lady who runs Juniper Hall in Surrey, is expecting a child and gossip cannot decide whether the father is the Comte de Narbonne or his friend Monseigneur Talleyrand. Even if that is not true, I know the bishop's current mistress is the widow of the Comte de Flahaut, who is bent on writing for a living.' Eleanor concluded her summary, warning Catherine that, however charming she may have found him, he would be of no use to her, and was certainly not to be trusted. Catherine assured Eleanor their meeting had been purely transitory and she would take heed of her advice. In actuality she was intrigued.

It was not until the autumn, though, that Mr Talleyrand made good his intent to call on her. She later learnt that it followed the departure of Mme de Staël for Switzerland which left him with no reason to visit the émigré community in Juniper Hall. Still, she was pleased he should remember her and accepted his invitation to visit the Ranelagh Gardens in Chelsea as a suitable neutral ground in which to become better acquainted with each other. He never walked without his cane and, thinking of the Dover dog owner, Catherine was inclined to think of him as another 'Peg Leg', or Piédcourt. His conversation interested her though. He had an amusing, if sardonic, take on people and politics, about both of which he was well informed. Unlike other émigrés, he was more discerning in his critique of the French government. Politics fascinated him more than any other man Catherine had known. His interest was more based on political theory than factional contests, and for once Catherine found herself fascinated by the topic. And the more she was prepared to listen, the more he enjoyed taking her for tea and little pastries in the Garden's rotunda.

It was not long afterwards that, on one of her visits to have tea with Eleanor, their conversation was interrupted by the footman announcing Mr Wickham. He apologised but had thought it best to tell them personally the sad news of the death of Mme Perregaux. Both ladies knew that Adèle had been ill for some time, but it was still a shock to hear she had succumbed to that cancer illness so young. Memories of her salon in rue du Sentier flooded back and Eleanor was visibly upset. Mr Wickham motioned Catherine out into the hall. It may not be the best moment but he was pleased to find her here and if she would not mind, could he have a word with her, he asked, ushering her into the dining room opposite.

He soon came to the point. 'I believe, Mrs Grand, that you have met Monseigneur Talleyrand,' he stated, deliberately using the bishop's form of address. Catherine was not surprised that Mr Wickham's business kept him so well informed. He went on to confirm that Monseigneur Talleyrand was on the Republic's list of proscribed émigrés.

'Surely that makes him more welcome here?' suggested Catherine.

'That depends,' replied Mr Wickham, 'on his intentions. After all, he has been a bishop who betrayed his church, an aristocrat who was among those who led the revolution and a peace envoy of a country that has made war on us. You understand our concern.' Catherine did not entirely recognise the picture he painted of the solitary émigré that she had met. Mr Wickham persisted: 'As with any foreigner, his overseas correspondence has to pass through the Aliens Office. That is the law. So I am aware he is on good terms with any number of personages across the Continent.'

Catherine was relieved to hear it and wondered where this was leading. He paused. 'Of course, he might ask an English lady to forward letters which would thus bypass the Aliens Office.' Catherine assured him she had not been so requested. She barely knew the gentleman.

'If he were to ask you, you would be doing me a service if you would allow us to see them at the Aliens Office.'

Catherine was shocked. 'You are not asking me to spy on him, are you?'

'Not at all; merely to act as his courier through us and so conform to the Law.' Catherine was distinctly dubious and it would have showed. Mr Wickham produced one of the new five-pound notes recently issued by the Bank of England.

'I would exchange this for each letter you passed on to me,' he promised. Catherine hoped this new paper money was of more value than the French assignats.

—⁓—

Catherine was not about to avoid Talleyrand solely because of the interest in him from officialdom. As Eleanor had told her, his main female companion was Mme de Flahaut, but Catherine was content to be alternative company for him on their occasional visits to the Ranelagh Gardens and listen to him analysing the events across the Channel. However savage the latest news, he was confident that terror tactics alone could not save Robespierre's government and he was confident of its inevitable demise, and that it was just a matter of time. At the Chinese pavilion he quoted to her the proverb 'With time and patience, the mulberry leaf becomes a silk gown.' Catherine was unsure whether he was referring to France or to himself. His confidence was infectious. She was reminded of Nat's expression 'We're survivors, you and me!' It was a happy time and only spoiled for Catherine when he told her that he hoped to leave for Switzerland soon. Catherine recalled that Switzerland was where Mme de Staël currently lived.

She saw less of him as the mild autumn gave way to a particularly icy winter, the worst winter since that of '88/89, they said. The freezing temperatures discouraged her from making her usual trips to the West End with Eleanor. The price of sea coal increased as the temperature decreased and Catherine strove to make her hearth fire last the way Ed had taught her in Dover. So she was surprised one December morning to find a heavily muffled Talleyrand on the doorstep inviting her to join him in visiting the Frost Fair that was being set up on the frozen stretch of the Thames. He had a cab waiting, the well-draped horse breathing little clouds into the icy air. She paused only to gather cloak, gloves and shawl. They were not the only ones. It seemed most of London had turned out for this rare opportunity to enjoy themselves on the ice between Blackfriars and London bridges. Any slip on the ice provoked hoots of laughter and no one begrudged the fancy prices charged by the stallholders. Of course, Piédcourt, as she now thought of him, took great care not to venture too far from a support of some sort, and Catherine soon guided him back to a stranded wherry boat whose owner was doing a roaring trade in mulled punch and sausages. The two of them exchanged amused comments about the antics of their fellow revellers. Catherine was delighted he had invited her on this adventure and realised she would miss him if he were to leave the country. So, she asked him about his move to Switzerland. He knitted his brow and admitted to her that it had been made clear to him that he would not be welcome there. Catherine was only slightly sympathetic but it was a reflective cab journey back to Kensington Square.

And then it struck her that perhaps she had been instrumental in this refusal of entry, by relaying a letter or two of his through to Mr Wickham. The more she thought her action may have precipitated his predicament, the more guilty she felt. A few days later, Charles Talleyrand was once more at her door. He had brought her a book of his, Miss Wollstonecraft's *A Vindication of the Rights of Women*. 'It didn't sell,' he told her with that sly grin of his. Catherine couldn't help but chuckle. On a more serious note, he told her that he had been visited by a couple of Mr Pitt's messengers who told him he was required to leave the kingdom within five days, and he was just getting rid of his last few books. Catherine felt her gut twist with remorse. He might have been in Switzerland by now. How could they treat him so? It was unreasonably short notice, unless they expected him to go to France and face the guillotine! He was appealing for more time.

'Where will you go?' she asked.

'Well, it is clear that none of the Coalition countries will have me. The problem is that to go further afield, America say, requires a lot more money.'

From what he had let slip about the poor proceeds from the sale of his library, Catherine suspected that he was not only without supporters here but was running short of funds. He was embarrassed to have mentioned it and was quick to imply he was on sufficient good standing with certain of the Whig aristocracy to be assured generous credit. Catherine was not convinced. She imagined that such a loan would be tantamount to paying a debtor to abscond.

Catherine slept badly that night. She remembered how she herself had felt when having to leave Calcutta for a strange destination, and in war time too. At least Philip Francis had paid for her exit and indeed had provided a fund to help her get established. Perhaps… she wondered, as an idea grew on her. It would be a form of reparation if he but knew it. She lit a candle and went to her escritoire desk to work out some sums. As the misty January dawn broke, she wrote a letter to Mr Wright.

When she next met Charles, he was quick to assure her he had secured an extension from Mr Pitt. He had also written copious letters to try to find out the cause of his banishment. 'Apparently my deportation had been requested by the Prussian and Austrian governments who seem to find it too disturbing to have a person spend his time correcting proofs of a novel!' Neither of them believed it but Charles was determined to put a brave face on it, especially as that day, 2nd February, happened to be his fortieth birthday. It was the right moment to offer him the funds he needed to take passage across the Atlantic. She would take no refusal and pressed on him a banker's draft to allow him to set up in that independent and neutral Republic. 'I suspect America is not the sort of place you would wish to arrive penniless.' He insisted it was a loan that he would repay it *coûte que coûte*. Eventually they sealed the contract more in the way of parting lovers than amicable business partners.

Although Catherine now had less to live on, she felt happier than she had for some time. It had been the first time that she had given, rather than received, subsistence from a man and it felt invigorating. She began to reason that her compliance with Mr Wickham's request had nothing to do with Mr Talleyrand's departure. It seemed he faced deportation anyway. She did not regret her act of charity but would like to be sure. So, she sought an interview with Mr Wickham to clarify it, only to be informed that he was unavailable, out of the country. It seemed unlikely but later Eleanor was able to confirm that one of the Craufords had met with him in Berne. Eleanor could not disguise her relief that Catherine would be free of that Talleyrand distraction and set about encouraging her to take the opportunity to meet more suitable male companions. It would be difficult saying it to Eleanor but Catherine was wary of becoming someone's mistress again, especially in England. It might be acceptable for certain of the English gentry, especially among those of the Prince of Wales's circle for whom such an appendage was *de rigeur*. But Catherine had long accepted that the doors of the English society ladies, on the other hand, would be ever closed to the likes of her and Eleanor. Fanny had explained that particular English prejudice long before.

It suited Eleanor, with Quintin away again on official business in Frankfurt, to have Catherine as a companion and they visited Hyde Park for its Rotten Row riders, the Haymarket for its theatres and Haydn's concerts, Drury Lane for opera and, naturally, Bond Street for its fashionable shops. Both ladies agreed that it was not the same as Paris had been to them before the revolution, but that Paris no longer existed, and at least here they were safe. Also, the latest fashion suited Catherine's tall figure. The long close-fitting skirt belted under the bosom emphasised her best features, while the cap allowed enough of her fair hair to tumble across her shoulders. 'You do not need any trimmings or trains,' said Eleanor approvingly as they prepared for another visit with her friends to Almack's in King Street where they could show off their expertise in the newly fashionable waltz dances. Several gentlemen were most attentive to them but, while Catherine enjoyed their attention, she could not take their frivolous conversation seriously and formed no attachments.

'I do not seem to be very good at being independent,' Catherine confided to Eleanor. 'The moment it is apparent there is no Mr Grand around, a man is interested in me for only one thing!'

Eleanor smiled in sympathy. 'They're not all like that.'

'I know: at least Talleyrand treated me like an equal. He was good company.'

'Well, he's in America and, let's face it, he did not ask you to accompany him. That's the price of being independent.' Catherine did not argue; Eleanor was judging from her own experience.

—⁂—

It was a beautiful warm summer and Eleanor invited her to visit Bath, a long-fashionable resort for those who, well, wanted to be fashionable. Catherine demurred. 'Surely it has become the preserve of those gamblers with more money than sense?' Eleanor had to admit it was a bit démodé these days. She suggested Tunbridge Wells instead, which was frequented by the more respectable members of society as well as being closer. Besides, 'No one who has lived in India would dream of drinking the water!' She would not listen to Catherine's refusal so that, in the end, Catherine had to admit her true reason was her need to economise. Eleanor was quick to offer to finance the trip, and was polite enough not to take the opportunity to upbraid Catherine for failing to find a suitable patron by now. Catherine was embarrassed but Eleanor began to plan to put her companion on a surer footing.

Shortly afterwards, Catherine received an invitation from Eleanor to meet at Christies' sale room in Bond Street in a couple of days' time. There Catherine found Eleanor was appraising the other buyers rather than the items for auction.

'He's here,' she said as they took their seats, leaving Catherine to guess to whom she was referring. Various items went under the hammer while Catherine was careful not to move a muscle for fear of appearing to bid. Then Eleanor nudged her as a bracket clock was bid for by an elderly gentleman a few rows further up.

'Bid for it!' she commanded. As Catherine duly obeyed she whispered, 'But we might get it.'

'Doesn't matter.'

She was soon outbid by the gentleman, to Catherine's relief. At the end of the auction, Catherine followed Eleanor who was making straight for the gentleman in question. She hailed him in Italian and, surprised, he replied in the same language. Eventually she introduced Mme Grand to him in French.

'This is the Marquis de Spinola, whom we knew in Paris. I have explained that you had the same interest in that bracket clock.'

He was obviously taken by Catherine; she was used to that. He was naturally sorry to have outbid such a deserving recipient of such a magnificent timepiece. Beauty deserves beauty and he would be delighted if she would accept it as a gift from him, and could he call on her to deliver it personally? Eleanora, as she was to him, gave her more appropriate Hanover Square address. It had worked as she had planned.

'Did you have to go through all that just to arrange an introduction?' Catherine asked.

'Oh yes. The Marquis now knows you to be a lady of discernment, while you know he is a generous gentleman of means, without having to take it further if you do not wish to.' Catherine sometimes wondered if Eleanor was too subtle for her own good. But, as Catherine discovered over the following weeks, she had chosen well.

Certainly Cristoforo Spinola was as good a conversationalist as Talleyrand, which was hardly surprising as he too was a diplomat, previously accredited to Versailles and now to St James. He was happy to explain to Catherine how the Genoa Republic differed from the French Republic. 'We have existed for centuries because we know how to trade.' Catherine thought of the sale rooms. 'You know King George has just become king of Corsica?' Catherine had read of the establishment of the Anglo-Corsican kingdom in defiance of revolutionary France. 'Well, I have been advising Mr Pitt, as it was us who sold Corsica to France only twenty-seven years ago. The Corsicans speak our language. We Genoese know how to broker a deal,' he said with some pride. 'This French Republic has no idea about trade. For example, it has killed off the *Compagnie des Indes*; literally – it guillotined its directors.' It prompted Catherine to think of the deliberate murder of her cousin Nicholas. Then, for the first time in ages, Catherine wondered about the community in Chandernagore. She shrugged off the memories, as Cristoforo finished his explanation and looked enquiringly at his silent companion.

'Britain knows how to trade too and it has a constitutional monarchy. Might not that suit France?' she asked, remembering Talleyrand's views.

'Ah, for that you need a monarch prepared to abide by a contract with the people's representatives, and the self-styled King Louis XVIII has just refused to do so.'

Catherine was keen to keep his attention and pressed him to define Genoa's position as a wise old Republic next door, so to speak, to a brash new one.

'We're strictly neutral,' he stated, 'but it is not so easy.' He was angry with Britain for entering Genoa harbour and snatching the French vessels that had taken refuge there after the fall of Toulon. But equally he was apprehensive at how rapidly the French republic had annexed Savoy and Nice the previous year. Piedmont was part of that same kingdom and was now the only buffer between Genoa and France. He sensed he was losing his audience.

'Enough of politics! May I be permitted to ask you to accompany me to Mr Sheridan's new Theatre Royal? I think you will enjoy Sarah Siddons' performance as Lady Macbeth.' Catherine readily accepted.

Hamburg

And so Catherine acquired a new patron. Cristoforo Spinola was a widower whose fluency in French resulted from twenty years in Paris. His English was still rudimentary so that Catherine's fluency in English went down well with his Mayfair staff, to which Marie, Catherine's Belgian maid, was added. Cristoforo was a considerate and convivial partner who reminded her more of her cousin Nicolas than her benefactor Lambertyre. Catherine was content. She would not consider it a loss of independence (she now acquired rent from her Kensington Square abode), merely a treaty between independent parties. Gossip might cavil at the goings-on of foreigners, she felt, but she could still hold her head high. The only former patron of hers still in England was Philip Francis and she suspected he would be far more concerned, depressed even, to find Mr Hastings had finally been overwhelmingly acquitted by Parliament of all the charges that he, Francis, had instigated all those years ago.

Of course Eleanor approved and Catherine now felt she could visit her on a more equal footing. As the autumn turned once more to winter, Catherine basked in the role of hostess to Cristoforo's gentlemen guests, such formalities being a far cry from the informal visit to the Frost Fair the winter before. At Cristoforo's dinner table she made easy conversation with whoever sat next to her. Her opening formula, 'Qu'est-ce que vous pensez de la politique francaise a ce moment?' was guaranteed to induce a loquacious, if not always interesting, response. However precarious the state of the latest French government, its army succeeded over the following nine months in defeating the coalition forces on every front. Belgium and the Netherlands were overrun, forcing the British contingent to leave Belgium via Hanover; Prussia made peace with France; Austria suffered a major defeat at Fleurus; Spain then made peace too and the Brittany counter-revolution was suppressed by General Hoche. This coalition had fallen apart and if Britain continued the fight at sea – and Cristoforo had been concerned at a naval battle in the bay of Genoa that spring – then the point of it was lost on Catherine. She was aware that Cristoforo's determination that Genoa should remain neutral did not endear him to the British government and he confided in Catherine that he was finding it difficult to get appointments with the relevant ministers. Oh dear, thought Catherine, at least Mr Pitt cannot expel an accredited ambassador the way he did Talleyrand.

That autumn Cristoforo told her how a fresh French government had been formed by the former comte de Barras following the suppression of a counter-revolution in Paris. 'Plus ça change, plus c'est la même chose,' quoted Catherine. She was more interested in the latest exhibition of young Thomas Lawrence's accomplished portraits at the Royal Academy, which she compared to the more flamboyant ones of Vigée Le Brun. She found herself surprisingly moved by the sombre *Fishermen at Sea* by an even younger William Turner. It seemed to match Cristoforo's increasingly dark moods. When, in the spring next year, General Bonaparte – the same twenty-six-year-old who had saved Barras's government the previous autumn – led the Army of Italy successfully into Piedmont defeating all before him, Cristoforo became as excited as one could expect of an ambassador and wrote to the Doge suggesting he be transferred to Paris to have access to whoever was the current foreign minister. Although the papers reported on the Piedmont armistice that put a cordon around Genoa, it was from Eleanor's Crauford network that they learnt that Bonaparte had promised the Directory a levy of several million francs on the republic of Genoa and neighbouring duchy of Parma. Cristoforo was now determined to get to Paris. It would not be easy but he told Catherine he would explore the best way they could achieve it, probably via Hanover.

While Catherine was flattered that he assumed she would accompany him, she was not keen to leave the security of London and her recuperating savings. She consulted with Eleanor, who reminded her of a similar debate when Tom Lewin had asked her to leave Paris with him. That was different, thought Catherine, as she fingered the silver ship pendant she was wearing round her neck. Eleanor felt responsible for this relationship but wanted to be sure of Catherine's priorities. Catherine was not in love with Cristoforo, was she? No, but she was a dozen years older now and, as she and Eleanor had discussed before, she needed a patron. To find a suitable replacement for Cristoforo would not be easy, even if it were desirable. Obviously, if she were to go, she would miss Eleanor enormously. Their companionship had restored Catherine's confidence and provided Eleanor with a delightful diversion.

They tried to view the proposition objectively. Paris was reported to be safer but also socially erratic and materially poor. Being an ambassador from a fellow republic should give Cristoforo some status and security but war-time revolutionary Paris could still be more threatening than exciting. In the end, it depended on how stable the latest French government, the Directory as it was called, would prove to be. They ended up agreeing that the best course of action was to stay a while in Hamburg and see how matters developed. Eleanor was aware that a number of émigrés were of the same opinion. Indeed, Mme de Flahaut, the one whom Talleyrand had tutored as a novelist (Catherine arched her eyebrows at that), had gone there from London on the arm of the Portuguese ambassador. 'Surely you mean "in the arms of"?' Both ladies laughed knowingly. If Cristoforo was unable to set up in Paris, he – they, rather – could always return to London. Finally, Eleanor mentioned that Jamie Crauford was stationed in Hanover and she would ask him to watch out for her should the need arise. It was a useful, and clinching, argument.

So Catherine agreed to sail with Cristoforo to Hamburg, having first drawn a banker's draft from Mr Wright, and tactfully taking the bracket clock with her. She had no difficulty encouraging Marie to be part of Spinola's entourage. Cristoforo secured their passage on the packet to Hamburg and, while not as large as an Indiaman, was at least better suited for passenger accommodation than Catherine had found on her previous voyages. It was a dismal, if safer, voyage across the German Sea and the squalls kept most of the passengers below until landfall was announced aloft. Even then, the steady rain obscured the banks of the Elbe estuary. However, as they neared Hamburg, Catherine was able to appreciate how busy the river was with many different vessels from a variety of mainly Baltic countries. Hamburg itself was a moated and walled city in a horseshoe shape on the north side of the river. Catherine had never seen anything like it, except perhaps that its imposing bastions reminded her of Fort William in Calcutta. It was certainly crowded. Catherine had expected the French émigré society there, but was astonished at how many other nationalities with their unfamiliar languages thronged the streets. Very different from London. She was glad to have Cristoforo arrange their lodgings.

His first task was to open an account with a local banker, Jacob Oppenheimer. Catherine was surprised that he should choose a Jew to handle his funds but Cristoforo assured her they were the best bankers in the Mediterranean. She trusted his judgment and later, privately, she followed his example. Her small draft was taken by Herr Oppenheimer's associate Moses Warburg rather than the great man himself, but Catherine did not mind being served by someone more her own age.

While Catherine set about writing to Eleanor, Cristoforo wrote again to Barras to obtain the Directory's authority for re-establishing a Genoese embassy in Paris. For months he got no answer to his requests and their 'temporary' lodgings in Hamburg seemed increasingly cramped. At least the summer was warm enough to enjoy their new surroundings and the variety of émigré businesses that had sprung up in the city. They took to strolling along the Jungfernsteig, Cristoforo to show off his beautiful companion and Catherine to view the change in fashions. The plainer attire of both sexes was a clear reflection of the effect of the Revolution on society, though the North German climate ensured more decorum in the ladies' dress than she heard was current in Paris.

Catherine decided to seek more informed news than available from local society and made an appointment with

James Crauford who was standing in for a fellow Scotsman, Mr Fraser, as Britain's official representative to the Hanseatic Cities. He was delighted to meet with her.

'Mrs Grand, I do not need your letter of introduction. I recognise you by the description from aunt Eleanor. If anything you are younger and prettier than she described,' he said graciously with more of a Scottish accent than Quintin's, she noticed. But then he had spent less of his younger years abroad than Quintin. She did not need to explain how she came to be in Hamburg with the Genoese representative; he already knew. He was aware of Spinola's predicament and was not that sympathetic. He took the view that it was for the British to command the seas while relying on Austria to contain the French Republic's new borders. However, as the former ambassador to The Hague, he could provide introductions should they succeed in passing through the Batavian Republic, as the new French client state was called.

—◌◌◌—

Mr Crauford kept in touch and he soon provided her with news that quickened her interest. In his latest letter to her, he mentioned that Monseigneur Talleyrand was in Hamburg, having obtained permission to return to France. Catherine was both surprised and pleased for him. His patience, and doubtless his persistent correspondence, had paid off then. She doubted Mme de Flahaut would distract him as she was rumoured to be totally taken up with her Portuguese lover. What would he find to do in Paris? she wondered. She resolved to meet him on as neutral a footing as seemed appropriate in the circumstances and suggested Cristoforo arrange it. Unfortunately, if Monsieur Talleyrand had arrived in Hamburg, none of the obvious émigrés had seen him, and he could not have stayed long. Indeed, a week or so later, Cristoforo learnt from the French newspapers that 'M. de Talleyrand-Perigord, the former bishop and privileged émigré had arrived in Paris.' Catherine was more disappointed to have missed him than she had expected to be, and it was nothing to do with her loan to him.

Mr Crauford was aware that Catherine and his aunt Eleanor had been part of the Perregaux salon and now approached her with a proposition.

'Forgive me for bringing this up, Mrs Grand, but while it would be impossible for the Marquis de Spinola to go to France without official authority, would you contemplate visiting M. Perregaux in Paris yourself, if it could be arranged?'

Catherine was both surprised and intrigued. Of course, it would have to have Cristoforo's blessing, but she would be doing Mr Crauford a service if she was prepared to deliver a confidential despatch to Lord Malmesbury who was currently en route to Paris to discuss peace terms. He would make it worth her while. It seemed innocuous enough. Catherine was bored with Hamburg. 'How much?' she asked.

He was amused. 'You would make someone a good wife.'

'I already am, unfortunately.'

'Ah, forgive me, I had forgotten Mr Grand.'

So had I, thought Catherine.

Cristoforo was pleased with the arrangement as she could also act as courier for his own letters. The three of them determined on her French persona. She was not on any émigré list but, just to be safe, she should be her sister, Mme Calnois, from Chandernagore. Aware of her interest in the contents, Crauford told her it was a confidential appraisal of the current status on the Meuse and Rhine fronts for Lord Malmesbury. As it might assist his negotiations, it was imperative he should receive them promptly and that they should not get lost or be opened by anyone other than the British delegation. It reminded her of Tom's Madras pouch. She was surprised they would trust her with something that important but Mr Crauford told her she had been vouched for by Mr Wickham.

'Welcome to the *Corps Diplomatique*,' he said.

'Return safely, my dear,' added Cristoforo.

More excited than apprehensive, she took four days by coach to the ancient frontier city of Nijmegen via Bremen, another free Hanseatic city, and Osnabruck. As Mme Calnois, she excited no interest at the border of the newly created French *départements* in Belgium and was easily able to obtain a place on the next public coach to the capital. Given what she had heard of the campaigns in recent years, she was not surprised to find the Belgian countryside still bore the scars, with branchless trees, few livestock and ungrazed pastures. The roads were particularly rutted and uncomfortable except in the immediate vicinity of a town. Even Brussels looked dilapidated and grim.

She expected better in Paris but was shocked to find the plundered aristocratic buildings desolate and the once-tidy side streets barely passable after four years without upkeep. She made her familiar way to rue de Mirabeau, which had been renamed again, this time as rue du Mont-Blanc, and to Jean Perregaux's latest home. He was absolutely delighted to see her. He himself had only returned to Paris less than a year previously and, he later admitted, had done rather well speculating in the latest paper currency. He asked after their mutual friends and indeed James Crauford who, Catherine was not surprised to hear, was another client of his. Catherine had to admit she was only visiting and was due back in Brussels in a matter of days. She was uncertain how much he knew of her mission. Never mind, he insisted she stay with him in the meantime. For Catherine to be staying on the same street that she had fled in terror four years previously was to finally lay to rest the ghost of that ordeal.

Jean deduced something of why she was in Paris and was able to direct her to the addresses she had been given. Rue du Mont-Blanc was not the only street to have been recently renamed. Irritatingly, that for Lord Malmesbury proved useless as he had insisted on relocating with his staff. She would follow it up the next day. That evening she dined alone with Jean and they talked about Adèle and old times. He also told her about the Clichy royalist faction's intent to get a majority of deputies sympathetic to their cause in next spring's elections. Personally he doubted it was viable, given the government's control of the election, and Catherine stored up his arguments so as to be able to repeat them to Mr Crauford as, no doubt, Jean intended. She asked after Monsieur Talleyrand. Jean had indeed been approached by citizen Talleyrand looking to sell his options on some land in Massachusetts, having failed to find a buyer in Hamburg. He added, studying Catherine's reaction, that Talleyrand was seen regularly in the company of a Mme de Brack. Catherine feigned disinterest. There was not much left for her in Paris. When she retired to bed she stared a long time at the remaining despatch for Lord Malmesbury. And then recalled the legend of Pandora's Box. It was best not to know. She duly delivered the confidential despatch next day. Lord Malmesbury was delighted to receive such a graceful young courier and was duly surprised to learn that young Catherine had accompanied Alan Fitzherbert, as he then was, on a similar mission back in 1782. Catherine did not pry into his prospects of securing peace now and was just glad to be relieved of the responsibility for delivering the despatch. She returned to give her thanks and a fond adieu to Jean before leaving for Hamburg by the same route she had come.

She and Cristoforo spent a miserable winter there while he exchanged frequent despatches with the Doge in Genoa. Mr Crauford had told Catherine of the failure of Lord Malmesbury's months-old peace effort following the French attempted invasions at Bantry Bay and later at Fishguard. Her interest in the outcome was solely the extent to which she and Cristoforo could resume the lifestyle of an ambassador. Alternatively, Catherine would have been content to return to London. Cristoforo's focus remained Continental, though. For the news that spring was dominated by the victories of the young General Bonaparte against the elderly Austrian generals sent to halt his advance through their Italian territory. Cristoforo could only fume at his enforced inability to protect his beloved Genoa's neutrality. In June they heard that Bonaparte had occupied the Venetian Republic, Genoa's ancient rival. It would seem the French Republic was not content to make war only against kingdoms.

'Catherine, I am thinking that we should go to France and apply for permits once there. Crossing the border proved easy enough for you, did it not?' he asked her.

'I am not sure. They would pay more attention to you at the border than they did to me as a single lady. What alias could you use?'

Cristoforo believed his diplomatic status should be enough and he could bluff the acceptance of his accreditation to the Directory. He was getting desperate to put his case to the government. She could be part of his retinue if she wished.

Catherine told Mr Crauford who was surprisingly supportive of the idea. He had only recently heard that the French wished to reopen peace negotiations, this time in Lille. It was more promising than in the previous autumn now that there were moderates in the Directory. Indeed, citizen Talleyrand had been appointed its Foreign Minister, though not one of the Directory. That's a remarkable feat, thought Catherine, for a penniless proscribed émigré. Mr Crauford continued confiding his hopes to his attractive, if distracted, listener: if Mr Pitt felt, now that Austria had made peace with France, that it would be an unduly expensive and less necessary business for Britain to continue alone, then Lord Malmesbury might yet be sent to Lille to negotiate a peace. If the Marquis was determined to get into France, this presented an opportunity. He now had Catherine's full attention.

Mr Crauford warmed to his theme. He suggested to Catherine that Spinola claim attendance as a delegate to the Lille peace conference. Why should not Spinola, who had advised the British government on its initial acquisition, represent Corsica, only recently abandoned to the French? It might seem a poor excuse but Crauford was aware the Dutch were also desperate to participate, and on as flimsy grounds. It would mean Spinola would have to be prepared to go to Lille but it should make it easier for him to get to Paris thereafter. Catherine thought Crauford was being remarkably keen that Cristoforo should succeed in crossing the border and was thus not unduly surprised when he asked if, in that eventuality, she might again act as his courier? It made sense to Catherine and she asked only, with a winning smile, that a contribution be made to their travel expenses. After all, if they need not return to Hamburg, Cristoforo would need to hire a coach for them to include her maid, his cook and manservant. Ever cautious, Catherine deposited her Wollstonecraft book and bracket clock with Herr Warburg at the same time as taking out some journey money.

It was with more confidence, then, that they arrived at the border at Nijmegen expecting to be able to continue to Lille in time for the peace delegation's arrival there. Cristoforo explained to the border guard that he was the Genoa Republic's official representative and was met with the shocking news that such a republic no longer existed.

'It is the Ligurian Republic now, by popular consent there. The Doge rules no more. Consequently you, Menheer Spinola, cannot be its representative!'

Cristoforo recovered quickly and used all his diplomatic guile to argue he was that republic's only possible ambassador and it was vital that he be able to attend the conference in Lille, but the border guard was adamant. He could not proceed. Catherine then took up her own – or on paper her sister's – cause. Already suspicious, the guard consulted with the list of émigrés and could find no reason to hold her. She was in a hurry to be on her way, conscious of the despatches entrusted to her care, but could not leave Cristoforo like this.

'What will you do?' she asked him.

'I'm not sure. It seems I am now stateless,' he looked at his few belongings on the coach, 'like so many others,' he added. 'Perhaps the Swiss Confederation will be more welcoming. For sure, I can assess the situation better from there. But don't worry about me; you carry on.'

He pressed a purse into her hands and gave her a last embrace, each promising to write whenever circumstances provided a definite address. Neither looked back as he went to redirect his coach and she to make her way, with Marie, to book a place on the public coach to Lille.

—⁓—

At Brussels, Marie asked to be released from Catherine's employ. Without their patron, Catherine doubted she could afford her and so readily agreed, paying the maid her due. She seemed to be making a habit of repatriating her maids. Accordingly, she was on her own when she arrived at Lille. Catherine was more nervous as she alighted at the coaching inn on the outskirts of this unfamiliar city. It too was walled with bastions but they were less imposing than those of Hamburg and Catherine noted that sections still had not been repaired from the siege by the Austrians a few years earlier. Hard cash was still a rare commodity in France and she had no trouble procuring a decent room at that inn by jangling a few coins. The French peace representatives – the same that had arranged the Peace of Basle with the Prussians a couple of years earlier – were already quartered in the city and Catherine had no difficulty learning of the intended quarters of Malmesbury's delegation.

Back in her room upstairs she looked for somewhere to hide her despatches. Ignoring the creaking floorboards as too obvious a cache, she placed them in the recess behind the shutters, breaking the seal in the process. Still, judging from the cobwebs, no maid ever cleaned there. It made her feel quite conspiratorial and she quite relished playing her sister's part as she waited ostensibly for 'news from her family in Paris'. It was with some relief that she was soon able to deliver the despatches to Lord Malmesbury personally as she had been instructed. He was delighted to meet her again and he paid her the compliment of advising her of the confidence he and Mr Pitt had in achieving an agreement this time with the more moderate French government now in place, albeit without disclosing how he intended to do so. Their discussion reminded Catherine of happy days in Paris all those years ago and wondered if they could ever be repeated.

It was a foolish hope. Before she had completed her arrangements for her onward journey to Paris, she learnt from the French papers of a sudden reversal of fortune for the negotiations. Apparently, there had been yet another coup d'état in Paris in which Barras, backed up by General Hoche's army, had had the leading moderates arrested and sentenced to deportation. The change was so sudden, it hardly seemed credible after the apparent waning of Jacobin influence recently. The new mood of the government was soon made clear in Lille: Lord Malmesbury's delegation was given a day to agree to the impossible and had to break off the negotiations.

Catherine had bad memories of a Jacobin Paris and toyed with the idea of attaching herself to Malmesbury's entourage on its way back to England. She had no idea how acceptable that would be. Hamburg held no allure and Spinola's hopes of rehabilitation were too much of a gamble. No, it would have to be Paris. She had no alternative. At least Jean Perregaux was expecting her. Perhaps Talleyrand had survived the purge of the moderates. She fervently hoped so. She made her arrangements for the next coach there. Being in charge of one's own destiny was proving difficult. Returning to Paris now was not so much a calculated gamble as the best of a limited choice of poor options.

Paris Again

Catherine woke with a start, conscious that the warmth of the fire had lulled her to sleep as she snuggled up in the comfort of the armchair. The firelight flickered in the darkened room and she realised it must be late in the night. She looked up at what had startled her and saw Talleyrand staring down at her. 'But it's Cathy' – he had always pronounced the English 'th' impeccably – 'my belle of Kensington Square! What a surprise! To what do I owe this considerable pleasure?' He took her hand and kissed it, looking into her anxious eyes.

'I'm so sorry; I must have fallen asleep.'

He did seem genuinely pleased to see her. He wore the official government regalia, a black coat with wide red lapels and embroidered cuffs and collar with a wide white silk sash. Catherine still wore the hooded cloak she had put on against the January cold. She stood up to take it off and put it aside as he sat down in the other armchair, watching her graceful movements with some admiration. She resumed her place and began her explanation.

'I was in Hamburg for a while,' she started. Talleyrand showed surprise.

'But so was I, last year. I had no idea. I thought you still in London.'

Catherine shrugged. 'It does not matter. It did not suit me; so I came to Paris three or four months ago and have lodgings in rue Nicaise.'

'That long! I wish I had known.'

'It was not easy. I had hoped to enjoy being in Paris again, now there is peace on our frontiers, but it's not the same. It's more expensive and everyone lives in fear. It's not so much the new taxes or the shortage of food, as it is that anyone can be suspected of treason for the slightest unwary comment. Where will it end?' Talleyrand nodded. 'Do not misunderstand me. I'm not coming to beg; citizen Perregaux has been kind enough to look after my affairs. No, I've come to you for advice.'

In truth, Catherine had come for more than advice. On a practical level, while Jean Perregaux had given her an advance against her Hamburg account, it would be convenient if Talleyrand remembered his debt to her of four years ago. On a more important level, though, she had heard that Mme de Staël, who had been Talleyrand's constant companion all this time in Paris, had been spurned by him at last. Catherine knew she was not the only lady drawn to him like a magnet but while Mme de Staël could act as his hostess for such functions as the grand ball, which he had recently held in honour of General Bonaparte, she had to be patient. She had learnt that from him. Now was the moment. She hooked back a stray curl and looked up at him hoping she showed more composure than she felt. She had rehearsed her purported purpose: so she explained how she found living in Paris a lot harder than five or six years ago and that consequently she was wondering whether she would be better off if she returned to London. However, she was concerned at the reports in the newspapers that General Bonaparte had been charged with invading Britain. She knew Charles to be not only well positioned to know, but also considerate enough to give her sensible advice. It sounded hollow now, but her Piédcourt chose to take her concern at face value.

He was happy to reassure her. He found young Bonaparte an exceptionally bright young man, too intelligent to think an invasion of England was remotely possible, and one who was aware that the Directory only wanted him as far from Paris as possible. Catherine encouraged him to elaborate. In his view Bonaparte was remarkable in being more a strategist than a mere soldier. He had rid the Mediterranean of the British Navy by the simple expedient of denying them any friendly port there and had agreed treaties, without recourse to the Directory, which had established peace on the Continent for the first time in four years. His treaty with the Austrian Empire showed remarkable restraint. He was the first republican whom Talleyrand had come across who did so. Catherine realised that these two, one a forty-four-year-old nonchalant diplomat, the other a twenty-nine-year-old dashing general, got on very well. It was reassuring to know since she had heard these past weeks how the foreign minister had only Barras as a friend in the Directory.

'But my dear Cathy, you must not think of leaving Paris. Especially now that I have found you. How can I forget your kindness when I was at my lowest ebb with no one to turn to? I shall be delighted to help you in any way I can. Believe me, I have become considerably better off since taking on this post. Better still, I can offer you my protection. After all, did we not enjoy each other's company while together in London? I know I did.'

They talked of those times and skirted over what had happened since. Catherine suspected he would have been aware how the Genoese ambassador had been refused entry to France but was unlikely to connect his companion 'Mme Calnois' with herself. For his part, Catherine noted, he managed to avoid mention of Mme de Staël, but he was happy to express pride in his hand-picked team here at the ministry, a newly completed hôtel on the rue du Bac in the fashionable Faubourg St Germain. Generally, he was well respected by the foreign ambassadors, though a small contretemps with the Americans over the price of his negotiation had alienated that fellow republic. He also hinted at the trouble he had with the misguided members of the Directory but in more gentle tones than, Catherine noted, Philip Francis had spoken of the Bengal Council. Eventually, he called to mind the time, much too late for her to go home, and said he would be delighted if she would spend the night here. Cathy, as she was now happy to be called, was delighted to accept.

—⁓—

She stayed a lot longer than one night. At his invitation she moved in and became more than just one of his team. Naturally, Cathy delighted in her new station with its lavish capabilities, but was careful not to let it go to her head. She was aware that Mme de Staël had assumed a role as Talleyrand's benefactor which, in the end, he found insufferable. And her rival had incurred the displeasure of General Bonaparte, whose views on women were decidedly provincial. Cathy was at pains to avoid the same fate. Having been hostess for the Marquis de Spinola, Mme Grand was well prepared for her role as the Foreign Minister's hostess, though it was on a far larger scale. She met so many people in a short time that her head reeled with the names and faces which she had to remember. She took her lead from Charles and paid particular attention to those whom he flattered. She was aware that she was the subject of curious gossip, but no more than were the other ladies of this parvenu society. Apart from the immoral behaviour that had become a common enough attribute of the liberated citizens of the republic, the key government figures were expected to have glamorous companions of chequered backgrounds. Catherine knew that General Bonaparte was an exception. Catherine was of the same age as Mme Bonaparte who had been a child bride in the West Indies as she had been in the East Indies. She hoped she was the prettier, even if socially she was only a mistress rather than a wife.

It was inevitable that they should meet. When they did, Joséphine drew her to one side away from the rest of the theatre-goers so as to have a tête-a-tête and satisfy their mutual curiosity.

'What was it like in India?'

Cathy had not been asked this before. 'It depends on the season. When the cool season came we had lots of fun. It's as if a year's entertainment was crammed into six months to make up for the waiting.' Cathy brought her hands together to mimic the short season and then threw them apart. 'The balls were magnificent. It was hectic. Sometimes George and I would take a boat a find a calm spot for a picnic to have a rest from it.' They were old memories. 'I was "Katy" then. It was a long time ago.'

Joséphine nodded. 'I was "Rose" then. I know what you mean.' Cathy asked her about Martinique and found her happy to recall those early years; no one ever asked her about her foreign childhood either.

'How do you find Paris?' asked Joséphine. Recalling the recent months by herself, Cathy admitted, 'It can be scary.'

'Really? Do you think so?' It was reminder of the difference between them. When they parted Cathy felt that at least she had an ally, if not a friend.

—∞—

She really looked forward to the time she shared with Charles. He was much busier than he affected to appear, reading and writing copious letters and reports. His official language was concise but when with her, he unburdened himself at leisure. The intimacy and trust in each other grew rapidly and Cathy dared believe this could be love. She wanted to write to Eleanor. She would be delighted for her. A letter to England might be difficult, though. At an appropriate moment she asked Charles, 'Do you have an Alien Office as they have in England, reading foreign correspondence?'

'Yes, of course. It's my *cabinet noire*. I get to read all post sent to foreign officials. It is vital for me to understand what they really think and intend. That, dear Cathy, is also my worth to Barras.'

'But if they know that, surely they avoid usual channels?'

'Naturally. However, the more likely coaches heading for the border curiously seem to be disproportionately held up by my highway "robbers"!' he chuckled.

She came to the point: 'And if I were to send a letter or two to my friends in England? Would they be intercepted?'

'Not if they were addressed to ordinary people,' he replied, a little more seriously.

Another time, after he had again mentioned how much certain Directors treated him so badly, she asked him why he was so disliked by the Directory. He was his usual relaxed self as he told her that they hated priests and nobles and he had been, of course, both. Besides, it was an animal instinct to fear, and therefore to hate, whatever it doesn't understand. Education should cure that. 'Sadly, Barras is the only educated member of the Directory.'

'Do you not mind, though?'

'Of course, but they need me and I like to think that I am useful to France's interests if I can occasionally act as a check on their more outrageous excesses.' She could understand that. He was forever toning down or delaying some of the more extravagant diktats of the Directory. What she had more difficulty understanding was why he encouraged Bonaparte's interest in an expedition to wrest Egypt from Ottoman control. Talleyrand, the believer in colonies rather than conquests, tried to explain its strategic and intellectual value but Cathy was more concerned that it would leave Charles without a valuable ally.

She was right to be concerned. No sooner had Bonaparte set off across the Mediterranean than there was a request that citizen Talleyrand be appointed ambassador to Constantinople. Cathy suspected its source was a rival for the Foreign Ministry, though it purported to be the wish of Bonaparte. The prospect appealed to neither of them. Cathy had met the Ottoman ambassador. He had been charming to her as the Foreign Minister's hostess, but she suspected she would be viewed very differently as a mistress in Constantinople. 'Have no fear, *ma chérie*, it will not come to that,' he assured her. But Cathy was worried enough to wonder if that meant only that she would be left behind. 'You should know me better than that,' he assured her, 'wait and see.'

Talleyrand prevaricated and fortunately the ship sent to collect him was captured by the British Navy, which had dared to re-enter the Mediterranean. The same fate befell the vessel due to take Mme Bonaparte to join her husband in

Egypt, so Talleyrand felt sure Bonaparte would understand his predicament. He made no effort to seek an alternative. It was a fortunate way out of what would have been a perilous post at the time that a French army was invading Ottoman Egypt.

Then the antagonism towards Charles became more personal. Returning from a visit to the Faubourg Montmartre, Cathy's cabriolet was stopped by two armed men in the familiar coloured uniform of a dark blue coat with a red collar and white lapels: the National Guard. They stepped up, squashed in either side of her, told her she was under arrest and directed the driver back across the river to the Temple Prison. Cathy was too shocked and frightened to argue.

Cathy knew nothing of prisons beyond the gruesome tales of the Terror of years previously. So it was a surprise to find The Temple, a tall multi-turreted fortress that she had only ever seen from the outside, was more like a hôtel inside. She was escorted to what seemed more an apartment than a cell and was told she could get anything in terms of food, books, writing materials or furniture even, as long as she could pay for such. It was small comfort. She was too fearful that Charles had suffered a similar fate. The guards were pleasant enough; apparently they already had two other English prisoners, Sir – they emphasised the 'Sir' – Sidney Smith and his secretary, Captain Wright, who had been held there for the last two years. It meant nothing to Cathy and she feared any communication with them might arouse further suspicion. She had been noticed, however, and her first decent meal from the guards was, she was told, courtesy of Sir Sidney Smith. She passed on her thanks to her gallant benefactor and awaited events with as much patience that she could muster while her anxieties mounted.

She tried to guess what had led to her arrest but could think of nothing she had done that could be viewed as anti-republican.

If her courier roles of the previous year as Mme Calnois had been known, she would have been arrested long before she moved to rue du Bac. Rather, she surmised, my arrest is in conjunction with an arrest of citizen Talleyrand, the suspect foreign minister. She spent a sleepless night worrying about him. The next day she borrowed the guard's *Journal de Paris* and was relieved to see no report of a change at the foreign ministry. It was frustrating as much as worrying. She was a handsome thirty-five-year-old and dreaded that all those years of effort were to end in such an ignominious manner, and for some unexplained crime which she was unaware she had committed. She was mindful of Nat Belcher's description of the crowds massing to see the guillotine do its work and shuddered. Out of sight from the door peephole, she knelt, crossed herself and prayed, the first prayers that she had made for many years.

Hamburg Again

Fortunately, her agonising ordeal only lasted a couple of days. To her surprise, the guards then announced she was free to go and she was escorted out to be met by Charles. They embraced, Charles nearly falling over his cane in his relief to be able to greet her again. She was trying to hold back her tears as much as her hair. He stammered for the first time. They urged the cabriolet to make good speed back to the Left Bank and home. Excitement spent, he explained what had happened.

When he had heard of her arrest, he was told that it was because she was a suspected English spy (that was old malicious gossip, she knew) who had written to London (Oh dear, thought Cathy, it had been intercepted after all) in a compromising manner.

'But all I wrote to Eleanor was that I loved you and hoped that we could be married!'

'I know and you don't know how much I was thrilled to hear that,' he said, 'but it also said something to the effect that you had not heard from Spinola and any intercepted letters from him might be compromising.' Charles raised one eyebrow at her, the way he could when expecting a rebuttal.

'Oh, Piédcourt, is that all? I was only concerned that my brief affair with Cristoforo might compromise my love for you in your eyes!' She dared not invite any other interpretation. Besides, he was clearly the target. If she was considered as being a spy, it would be easier to accuse Talleyrand of being in the pay of England and have him executed or deported. The extent to which her letter had been used to get rid of the Foreign Minister scared her. 'What did you do?'

'I doubt very much that they were aware that you have spent time in London and Hanover recently. So I told Barras your connections were with India and that you could not possibly be involved in any such English intrigues. I also appealed to him to understand how much I loved you! He showed my letter to the other four members of the Directory and you can imagine what fun they had at my expense. Barras says they were all for investigating you and having me dismissed as a suspected traitor, but he was able to smooth things over, for now at least, and have you released.' She asked if he knew who was responsible. He shook his head. 'I have a suspicion; but any one of the other members of the Directory could wish me dismissed. It is impossible to be sure. The important thing is that it failed.'

However reassuringly he explained the outcome, it had been a narrow escape from the sort of arbitrary punishment that the Directory had meted out to hundreds of others on just as flimsy an excuse. Charles had warned her from the beginning that his enemies would include her in their insulting insinuations, but she had not expected it to include treason. He now advised her to allow them to think she was as empty-headed as she was beautiful. She should let her thoughtfulness be taken as ignorance. Playing the fool had saved the Roman emperor Claudius from assassination, as he put it. Cathy was initially upset at being asked to adopt such a role, but then was mindful of how the ladies of the Perregaux salon had cautioned in like manner: mask your mind and flaunt your figure!

The other precaution they discussed was how to deal with her status as the wife of an Englishman. She confirmed to Charles that she had indeed been properly married to Mr Grand in both Protestant and Catholic ceremonies. The best they could do was secure a divorce on the grounds of his being out of touch these past twenty years under the Republic's new divorce laws. So that she did. Her marriage to George was annulled, at least as far as the State was concerned, within days. While it reduced the government's ability to label her 'English' it did not advance the couple's ability to get married, at least in a church. Some of those parish priests that had accepted the Republican constitution, and thus been excommunicated, had since got married. Cathy was aware, though, that deep down, her Piédcourt believed his bishop's vows had put him beyond that.

And so they continued to behave like a married couple in all but name. It was unavoidable that she should remain 'Mme Grand' and she was careful to act as an unassuming and pleasant hostess to the many dignitaries that visited the ministry. He too was playing a role, affecting a composure she knew he did not feel as the pressure on him mounted. His efforts to promote understanding among the foreign representatives in Paris were contradicted by the Directory's choice of arrogant ambassadors to their home countries. He managed to get a particularly high-handed one, Joseph Fouché, removed from Milan, only to find him appointed to The Hague. The failure of trust in diplomatic circles culminated in a second coalition of allies against the Republic. However frustrated Charles was with the government's hubristic foreign policy, he was privately furious that spring when, ignoring him completely, his masters in the Directory stupidly declared war again on Austria despite their under-resourced armies being incapable of inflicting any damage on their enemies. Inevitably, they were beaten back on every front. Equally inevitably, the Directory found it convenient to make citizen Talleyrand the scapegoat for its failures. The papers were merciless in their criticism of him.

Cathy knew their position was precarious and that Talleyrand only carried on to ensure he had adequate funds when the inevitable fall occurred. Her own Hamburg banker, Herr Warburg, had set up his own business and she advised Charles to transfer his spare wealth to that safe haven. The Batavian Republic's border was the only one not caught up in the disastrous war. So it would be possible for her to travel in relative safety through there to Hanover. That July, when Fouché, who would not have forgotten who was responsible for his losing the lucrative Milan position, was appointed Minister of Police, Charles sent in his resignation. It was only two years since he had secured the post. They moved out of rue du Bac to a street, rue Taitbout, not far from her earlier life on rue du Mont-Blanc, back in the Faubourg Montmartre.

Without the constant pressure from the Directory, let alone foreign affairs, Charles became much more relaxed. It was a warm summer with only occasional showers so they took to taking cabriolets out to explore the suburbs. Charles still cautioned her to be on her guard. Fouché was proving to be efficient in rooting out any influential critics of the Directory, Jacobin or Constitutionalist. So, bearing in mind Cathy's suggestion, Charles took an interest in the situation on the north-east border. The latest ambassador to Berlin, Sieyès, a more capable one than most, was doing a good job of keeping

Prussia out of the war, and thus the Rhine border quiet, though the English were pressing it to join this second coalition through a Mr Crauford.

'Crauford?' asked Cathy in surprise.

'Yes, Mr Quintin Crauford. Do you know him?'

'Why yes,' she replied with relief. 'He was part of the salon Perregaux back in '83.'

It was not the time to let him know of her more recent contact with a member of that clan. Rather, it seemed as safe a time as any to secure a portion of his savings beyond the Republic. They hoped Cathy would not be under surveillance now that he was no longer a minister. Accordingly, equipped with bankers' drafts, she took the road to Nijmegen and Hamburg, delighted at the trust he had placed in her.

—⁂—

Sir James Crauford, as he was now titled, was as pleased to see her as she him, and offered to put her up while she was in Hamburg. He knew of her partnership with citizen Talleyrand, of course, and even knew of her time in the Temple Prison. Sir Sidney Smith was one of his correspondents, he admitted. Cathy was quick to pass on her precious drafts to Moses Warburg who assured her that citizen Talleyrand could count on his total discretion and investment security. Feeling much relieved, she returned to enjoy Crauford's hospitality, from which she could safely write to Eleanor and even to Fanny Chambers since Sir James Crauford, ever in touch with the East India Company's affairs, had mentioned Sir Robert Chambers had retired back to England only a month or so earlier. Despite his enjoyment of her company, her host, as tactfully as he could, advised her to hurry back to Paris.

The reason became obvious the following day. The papers carried the news of the Duke of York's landing with a combined British and Russian force on the north of the Batavian Republic. Cathy was to hurry or she would be cut off by the advancing army. Sir James Crauford provided her with an English testimonial in that event, recommended hiring a post-chaise rather than the more comfortable but slower public coach and wished her God speed. Her confidence dented, Cathy hurriedly took the familiar route towards Nijmegen. Could she ever be free of worry? The possibility of being reported on by the French Republic's agents in Hamburg was but a small threat compared to being cut off from Paris and her one love.

She suppressed her concerns and decided to view this escapade as an adventure. As she approached the Dutch border, people were more concerned to leave the Republic's war zone than enter it and her vehicle struggled to get through the one-way stream of traffic. Once within the city limits she left the post-chaise for others and asked to be recommended a reliable horse dealer. It would be the first serious riding she would have done since a few graceful turns around Hyde Park but it should prove a more flexible way to avoid the converging armies before hostilities commenced. She found a suitable size of boy's riding breeches and boots and exchanged her feathered hat for a more weatherproof tricorn. Not bad, she thought, as she packed her hand luggage into her new saddle bag. If Sarah Siddons can play Hamlet, I can play Dick Turpin. Thus appropriately dressed, she bought a mare that looked to have more stamina than looks, or that was what the dealer assured her. He was not wrong. She stuck to the main road to avoid getting lost and frequently had to move aside for the commissariat wagons heading north. She noted that, after seven years of war, the army was a well-practised and orderly machine. She arrived safely in Brussels and found an inn that proved efficient in looking after the needs of her and her mount. Having carefully consigned her testimonial from Sir James Crauford to the fire, she made her way more confidently southwards to Paris. Within three days she arrived, tired and aching, certainly, but well proud of herself.

If anyone had reported on her movements, no action was evident from the authorities. And her Piédcourt was delighted to have her safely back and her mission a success. While he no longer had an official position, he continued to cultivate his contacts and assess the capabilities, or lack of them, of the Directory as its armies retreated in Italy, Switzerland and Germany. As with the rest of Paris, he wanted to know the progress of Bonaparte in Egypt but the British Navy had effectively cut them off from any news of that expedition. It did not bode well. As Charles put it, 'The Directory is incapable of directing!' He had met with the Abbé Sieyès, recently made a member of the Directory after his success in Berlin.

'I think Paul Barras is hedging his bets by accepting such a well-known constitutional monarchist into the Directory,' he told Cathy, 'but it makes a change to have a man of intellect among them.'

'I thought the Revolution has no need of *savants*,' quoted Cathy.

'Quite right, *chérie*. They can only ignore him, which is just as well as he has designs on them.' Charles was amused. 'You can tell Abbé Sieyès was trained by Jesuits. He may have a plan to remodel the Directory and the Constitution but it is hopelessly convoluted in design.' She knew her Piédcourt was waiting as usual for a turn in events.

Then, suddenly, rumours spread of Bonaparte's impending return. Before he even reached Fréjus the news had invigorated the country, helped by victories at last over the coalition forces at Castricum in Holland and Zurich in Switzerland. Talleyrand was delighted at the opportunity that his hero's return offered but also expressed his nervousness to Cathy.

'I'm not sure he will trust me.' He told her why. 'I lent him 100,000 francs for his Egypt expedition. It was kindly meant but, given my position vis-à-vis the Directory at the time, he may suspect ulterior motives.'

'Surely not. Not everyone thinks the way you do.'

'On the contrary, I am sure he does!' Still, Talleyrand needed to talk to him. As he confided to Cathy, Bonaparte could be the person to precipitate the sort of change needed for the country's government.

Suitably buoyed up, Talleyrand was the first would-be conspirator to visit Bonaparte at his home around the corner in the recently renamed rue de la Victoire. He returned many hours later and Cathy thought that if his club foot had allowed, he would have had a spring in his step, so pleased was he with the meeting. He did not tell her what was discussed – it was likely treasonable – but merely told her that, on his voyage back across the Mediterranean, Bonaparte had included in his reading a biography of Oliver Cromwell. The reference was not lost on her.

From then on, matters progressed at a pace. At times Cathy found the rue Taitbout as busy as the rue du Bac. A frequent visitor was the Abbé Sieyès. Bonaparte also walked round to the rue Taitbout to save Talleyrand's awkward gait, though never at the same time as Sieyès. Occasionally Charles would make the short trip to rue du Mont-Blanc where General Moreau held court. Once Cathy was surprised to be introduced to Joseph Fouché. Charles later reassured her, 'We need to know his intentions; he is too powerful to ignore.'

'But can you trust him?'

'Probably not. He will back whoever holds the strongest cards, and it is up to us to convince him we do.'

By the end of October, Charles felt confident enough to tell Cathy what was being hatched. 'You remember I said Abbé Sieyès wanted the Directory and the Constitution to be remodelled to his design? Well, I had not realised that he had hoped to lead a coup in order to do so. He needs military support of course and had expected General Joubert to be the one. But he was killed in Italy a few weeks ago. He then turned to Jean Bernadotte, the minister of war. But, surprisingly, Bernadotte is sitting on the fence and hopefully will remain there. So it has been easy for me to convince Abbé Sieyès that Bonaparte is the obvious choice. Bonaparte himself wants this to be a swift and bloodless coup if possible. He has learnt from the 13 Vendémiaire massacre.'

'Is that possible?' Cathy asked nervously.

'It depends on the preparation beforehand.'

'And you will be party to this?'

Charles nodded. 'Bonaparte has the support of Moreau and his troops, but he does not have sufficient political connections. The key obstacle will be Barras. Sieyès cannot handle him. So, knowing my relationship with Paul, Bonaparte expects me to deal with him. It's a dangerous proposition. Paul could as easily have us all guillotined the moment I broach the matter of Sieyès' proposals.'

'I thought you got on with Barras. After all, he was the one who had me released from prison and refused to prosecute you. What will you do?'

'I know and I hope he will go quietly. He has mentioned he found the burden of state heavy at times. I shall have to convince him he can go without retribution. Paul loves money – don't we all – so a massive bribe might buy his retirement. But I fear it may not be enough, and Bonaparte has made it clear he needs no martyrs if at all possible. It will be a delicate negotiation.' While he thought about it, Cathy called for some wine. They waited in silence while the manservant brought a bottle, opened it, put another log on the fire and discreetly left the room. Cathy poured out a couple of glasses, handing one to Charles.

'I think I can help.'

'Really? How?'

She leant forward towards him and lowered her voice. 'I came across one of Lord Malmesbury's despatches a couple of years ago.'

'Came across?' he asked in surprise.

'Never mind how, but there was something in the contents that might be useful.'

Charles was all ears. 'This was a despatch from Lord Malmesbury?'

'No. To him, from Hanover.' She could see how he was piecing together her time with Spinola in Hamburg and how the reference in the letter that had led to her arrest might not have been that innocent. She hurriedly continued: 'It was in Dutch, though. That's the second language of both Crauford and Malmesbury. But Barras was mentioned in it.'

'But it was in Dutch?'

'Yes.' Charles's exasperation began to show, but Catherine wanted him to concentrate on the contents. 'I attended the weekly church service on board the *Zeeuw* and came to know some Dutch, in particular their Pater Noster.' The ex-bishop nodded. 'The bit about Barras was similar to *en vergeef ons onze schuld, zoals ook wij aan anderen hun schuld vergeven*. He was asking or being offered a royal pardon.'

'Are you sure?'

'Well it certainly read like that.'

Charles was thoughtful. It could be possible. At that time Barras would have been seriously afraid that the moderates might take over. He certainly wouldn't want it known now. Yes, a hint that we do know might just be the leverage – the final tipping point – that we need. 'Deo gratias! Dearest Cathy, you're an angel!'

Neither of them spoke of it again and Cathy was grateful not to be involved further in his political deliberations. The less she knew, the better. But, not long after, Charles told her she should have a travel bag ready packed.

'Oh, why?'

'Just in case I do not return home tomorrow.'

'Where would I go?'

He could not answer that and Cathy chose to ignore his request. The next morning he gave her a particularly fond lingering farewell before leaving for rue de la Victoire. Cathy waited anxiously, conscious of the uninterrupted calm of the nearby streets.

Fortunately, he did return late in the day and told her how he went on from Bonaparte's hôtel to visit Barras at the Luxembourg Palace, which was ringed with Moreau's troops. He left there with Barras' letter of resignation in his pocket. The rest of the coup d'état only succeeded with the intervention of Bonaparte's brother, Joseph. But succeed it did and the Directory was replaced with the Roman-style Consulate of Sieyès, Bonaparte and another. Citizen Talleyrand could look forward to being back as Foreign Minister. Cathy was delighted. Not only did they move back to hôtel Gallifet in rue du Bac, but Charles could barely conceal his delight at having made a tidy profit selling government stock that he'd bought only days before the coup. That's my Piédcourt, thought Cathy!

Neuilly

Cathy had total confidence in Charles's judgement and was not at all surprised when his predictions about Bonaparte came to fruition. The First Consul, as Bonaparte was now styled, lost no time in setting up a form of civilian government which avoided some of the more onerous checks and balances that Sieyès had expected to instigate. Sieyès realised his General Monck had become a Cromwell and wisely, and expensively, followed Barras into retirement. In his place, Bonaparte appointed Cambacérès, a most able lawyer who, Cathy had been told by the gossips, preferred men to women. The new Roman-style structure of Consulate, Tribunes and Prefects prompted Charles to label the Consulate as 'Hic, Haec, Hoc'. He had to explain it to Cathy. 'It's the Latin declension of "He", "She" and "It".' She had less trouble allocating the description to the members of the revised Consulate. There was no question of their ability, though, as they set about reforming every aspect of the government, bringing in representatives of every shade of political opinion. No previous coup had been so deliberately tolerant. As Charles told her, the key policy of the First Consul was to convince and consolidate the French people. He relied on

Talleyrand to propose those former royalists and moderates that he could vouch for.

They were heady days. When Bonaparte set up a Banque de France to help stabilise the finances, it was Jean Perregaux who was appointed the key governor of the new institution. Of the many dinners that Cathy was hostess to, the one for her friend Jean was her most enjoyable. As foreign minister, Talleyrand was involved in spreading confidence among the ambassadors, a confidence that was reflected in the strengthening value of the franc. Bonaparte wrote personally to the Austrian Emperor and King George proposing peace. It was the British Foreign Secretary, another Lord Grenville, who replied to Talleyrand, evidently to snub Bonaparte. Grenville's reply was that peace was conditional on the restoration of the French monarchy. As Charles put it, 'On that basis, they should allow the restoration of the Stuarts to the British throne! No, it is clear that they believe we are still too weak and fractured to last any longer than previous administrations. They simply do not understand. The Revolution is over; the Republic is being consolidated.' Cathy realised that, as a poor exile in republican America, he had appreciated the difference more than the wealthy aristocrats in England could. 'But will it last?' she asked, knowing how closely their future was tied to it. 'Well, it must! It certainly has the right ingredients this time,' Charles replied with deliberation.

In a matter of weeks over that winter, the Consulate tackled law and order, even advising the police not to harass returning émigrés. While the First Consul set about dazzling the people with reliable local justice, his Foreign Minister bought a villa in Neuilly large enough to entertain, and thus win over, the great and the good of the various factions. His most lavish ball was given on the 14th July, now a public holiday, in honour of the

First Consul, returned as the heroic victor over the Austrians at Marengo only weeks earlier. Cathy was shocked to hear that Mme de Staël had asked to be invited and was greatly relieved when Charles said she had been refused, though Cathy was aware that might just as easily be to avoid irritating Bonaparte, the guest of honour, than to spare her having to entertain her rival. There were plenty of other tensions but, however much recent history made the guests suspicious or bitter towards each other, such feelings were suppressed in the general wish to be part of the New Order. Cathy was well aware of the political importance of these entertainments and played her part in correctly flattering both the nouveau riche and the amnestied aristocrats, even if she knew some of them would privately malign her as that 'mistress from the Indies'. Many of the men had reverted to some extent to the sort of clothing associated with the ancient regime while the ladies wore the alluring, if scanty, 'Roman' clothing made recently fashionable: flimsy gowns à la Diana, tunics à la Minerva, and buskins à la Ceres. The candlelight reflected from every size and type of gem extravagantly worn by them. Cathy herself was careful not to take it too far for fear of being seen as another Mme Tallien, who had been labelled 'Government Property' for her succession of lovers. Cathy craved respectability for herself. If Charles was going to invoke the extravagant lifestyle and prestige of his ancient aristocratic lineage, then she was not going to let him down. She would show them.

Between her and Charles, they had worked out a system to improve their income. For those who wished to avail themselves of the influence of the foreign minister, he set the fee and it was Cathy who ensured that the discreet payment was duly paid for even the promise of his services. It was the custom, though the amount sometimes surprised. It allowed the Foreign

Minister to be a lavish and popular host as well as adding to his salary. One of their investments was a little chateau in the village of Sains-du-Nord near the former Belgium border and Cathy was made joint owner on the title deeds. From her own property here, of course, she could more readily travel across to Hamburg without exciting undue interest from the newly efficient gendarmerie. The attempt to assassinate Bonaparte the previous winter had been a reminder that they needed to have their savings secure should another attempt succeed. It had been a near thing. Charles and Cathy were already at the Opéra when they heard the explosion. Moments later, Bonaparte arrived as if nothing had happened, to be greeted by applause from the relieved audience. Cathy had noticed that Joséphine was still picking splinters out of her cashmere shawl as Haydn's *Creation* came to its end, though.

'Cathy, my dear, I have a letter here from a Vicomte de Lambertyre.' Cathy settled her nerves as she went through to join him. 'It says, most politely, that he is looking to be recompensed for the loss of his belongings back in '92 and mentions that you would know about it.'

Cathy took it coolly. 'Yes, I remember him. He was on rue de Mirabeau, rue du Mont-Blanc as is. Does he not know that émigrés may return on condition they do not seek to reclaim their confiscated property?'

Charles smiled up at her. 'That rather depends on who did the confiscating. He is suggesting that it is you who owes him the value of certain goods.' She pulled a face without answering.

'Don't worry, I can always send him away with a flea in his ear.'

Cathy thought about it; they could afford to settle with him. It would be worth it to bury that part of her past. 'How much?'

'Ah, now we are talking business. Let me suggest to him it was half what he asks?'

'No,' she would rather make decent reparation and ensure no more was said. She suggested an alternative. 'Can you not rather answer something to the effect that we are happy to support a French nobleman known for his discretion and would be prepared to provide him with a reasonable annuity? That way he knows it would cease if he were to talk about it.' Charles was delighted.

'What a team we make!' They agreed an amount and Cathy breathed a sigh of relief.

—⁂—

Cathy did not always have to rely on Charles for her to keep up with foreign affairs, so swiftly did good news spread. For, that autumn, the second coalition began to break up as its forces were beaten back on every front, indeed almost to the gates of Vienna. The remnants of the Russian army retired to Russia and the Tsar fell out with Britain as much as with Austria. Once more England was left the only country at war with France. Pitt, the British Prime Minister, resigned, ostensibly over Catholic Emancipation, and his successor immediately announced he would make peace. It was an associate of Sieyès, Louis Otto, who was already in England as Superintendent of French Prisoners, who was authorised by Bonaparte to open negotiations, without consulting Talleyrand.

When Cathy asked him about this, Charles appeared his usual nonchalant self. She knew him better. Nevertheless, he reminded her how Bonaparte had concluded peace with the Austrians in '97 without recourse to the Directory and he doubted there would be much in his current dealings that he would disagree with. Indeed, after eight years of war, France was in a stronger position than ever and Bonaparte could enforce a Pax Gallica in the same way that his hero, Caesar, had enforced a Pax Romana. When Bonaparte reacquired Louisiana from the Spanish as the price of restoring the Naples kingdom to the Bourbons, it accorded well with Talleyrand's belief in colonies rather than conquests. For all these noble sentiments, Cathy was aware of his regret at the lost opportunity for prestige, let alone further commission.

Yet, not long after, Bonaparte entrusted his foreign minister to ensure the Italian deputies agreed his new constitution for the Cisalpine Republic. The deputies were summoned to Lyons where Talleyrand lavishly entertained them and secured their cooperation within a few weeks. He confessed to Cathy that he had found Lyons in a dreadful state having suffered terribly from the previous republican regimes. So he had spent further time there rebuilding the silk trade for which it once had been famous. Raw silk from newly annexed Piedmont now went west to Lyons rather than east to Lombardy. Cathy was pleased to find a new, more generous, side to her Piédcourt.

The only negotiation that Charles was annoyed not to be involved in was that which Bonaparte was carrying out with the Papacy. Talleyrand, the ex-bishop, had been one of the prime proponents of confiscating church property and having the clergy subjected to the republican constitution a decade previously. So they both understood why Bonaparte preferred to keep him out of a negotiation to restore the Catholic Church to France and thus heal one of the deepest grievances of the Revolution. Cathy was aware that his frustration at not being involved in the negotiation was also on a personal level.

For they still wished to be married. Cathy had become used to being introduced as Mme Grand to visiting dignitaries and was aware that some of their wives took exception to being introduced to the Foreign Minister's mistress. That was hurtful but not unbearable. Marriage for Cathy was not only for external show but also a cementing of the loving relationship that she and Charles had. She had told him openly, if he had not already known, that she did not seem able to conceive children and he had comforted her with words and an embrace, knowing how sore a topic it must be for her. They even discussed the possibility of adopting a child. He knew that Mme de Genlis had done so; the girl in question was now Lady FitzGerald.

'Besides…'

'Besides what?' she asked.

'Oh, nothing. I was just thinking that procreation need not be the fundamental basis of marriage these days.'

'You were going to say something else.'

'Was I? Well it doesn't matter.'

Cathy was sure it did, but knew he was not prepared to say so now. She knew he trusted her and so she would trust him. If he already had a child by a previous mistress, he likely did not wish it known, not least for the child's sake. As for marriage, she knew that he still felt his bishop's vows were an impediment personally, even if publicly he had long shrugged them aside. However, they could be annulled by a Pope and Bonaparte's willingness to do a deal with the new Pope offered an opportunity. But only if he could be involved in the negotiations.

Bonaparte had been encouraged by the new Pope, Pius VII, who prior to his election had made a point of declaring Christianity compatible with equality and democracy. Given the delicacy of the issue in republican France, negotiations had started in secret led by Joseph Bonaparte and the papal Secretary of State Ercole Consalvi. It was several months before an agreement was reached on a Catholic Church in France, paid for by the State but without its former property. Its hierarchy would be drawn from Constitutional as well as Non-constitutional clergy proposed by Bonaparte in a way that mirrored his Prefects' appointment and structure nationally. It was natural to Bonaparte that the head of his restored French Catholic Church should be Talleyrand and he proposed that he be made a cardinal in the same way that Cardinals Richelieu and Mazarin had served the French monarchy. It would be extraordinary if the Pope was prepared to promote the renegade Bishop of Autun, the founder of the schismatic Constitutional church, but Napoleon was prepared to gamble that the prize of restoring France, Belgium and, by extension, the occupied Italian states, to the Church would be worth it.

Cathy was immediately impressed. It would put Charles head and shoulders above Bonaparte's other ministers. It was Charles, however, who explained his disinclination. Apart from the likelihood of the Pope's disagreement to the proposal, it would make it impossible for him to be married. He would rather put the prospect of being married above the prestige of being Bonaparte's cardinal. Cathy was stunned by such an affirmation of love for her. She had not asked for this test of his devotion and, whatever pleasure it gave her, it raised a concern that she shared with him. For, to refuse this gift would be to risk the displeasure of Bonaparte, whose studied tantrums and their repercussions were already feared. Talleyrand the diplomat reassured her that he could convince his patron that to push for the cardinal's hat would be a step too far in the negotiations. He would work on the alternative.

So, with the Concordat near completion, Talleyrand intervened. Could not the draft Concordat give absolution to those Constitutional clergy who had got married? Bonaparte agreed it was only fair, another compromise in the spirit of reconciliation. But it was flatly rejected by the papal representatives and they broke off the negotiations. Bonaparte was furious with his foreign minister for allowing this extra clause to upset a conclusion that he badly wanted. He made his displeasure known in no uncertain terms. Cathy listened patiently to Charles unburdening himself each evening. It was a measure of how much he realised that he had overplayed his hand, that he suggested that they visit the spa at Bourbon l'Archembault, in the centre of France and a safe distance from the capital. Cathy found it nothing like fashionable Tunbridge Wells but its tranquillity suited them. Here in rural France they relaxed and had time only for each other. It was, thought Cathy, the real, if increasingly rare, Talleyrand, free of mercenary intrigue and happy to wait upon events to sort themselves out.

Sure enough, in the absence of his awkward minister, Bonaparte was able to resume negotiations directly with Consalvi and conclude the compromises to mutual satisfaction. The Concordat included a clause which gave absolution to priests who had broken with the Church and had married. But no such amnesty was forthcoming to those who had taken monastic or bishop's vows. Thus Talleyrand had been personally thwarted, but Bonaparte was content with that; he could now concentrate on getting the backing of the more anti-clerical members of his army and government.

Bonaparte had readily forgiven his Foreign Minister for delaying the Concordat but still did not include him in the finalisation of the treaty with England.

'Does he not trust you?' asked Cathy anxiously. Her Piédcourt sought to reassure her with a smile. It may simply be Bonaparte's concern to avoid his producing another extra clause that would further delay it.

'Mind you,' he told Cathy, 'the preliminary treaty is good enough. France now has natural borders up to the Rhine and the Alps and our former colonies restored. My only fear is that, having gained nothing, Britain may be sufficiently humiliated to try again.' Cathy was reminded of the negotiations to bring about the end of the previous war.

'It is so easy to make war and so difficult to make peace,' she mused. 'I remember in '83 it took months and months to accomplish and there were willing parties involved then too.'

'That is true, though I am surprised you remember it,' he said and, without waiting for her to comment, went on: 'Usually Bonaparte gives deadlines at the point of a sword and an armistice quickly follows. This is slightly different with an ocean or two involved.'

Charles saw her thoughtful expression and tilted her chin up. 'For the moment, though, we are certain of peace and that deserves a celebration!'

She readily agreed and he asked the butler for a bottle of champagne.

—·—

By now, Jean Perregaux, in anticipation of a formal treaty, was already in communication with his English clients who had had to wait nearly a decade to access their funds with him. From Jean, Cathy learnt of the intention of Philip Francis to visit Paris with his family when that became possible. It raised uncomfortable memories and she hoped that he no more wished to meet her than her him. With any luck she might happen to be taking the waters at Bourbon l'Archembault at the time. On the other hand, she received a long letter from Fanny who brought her up to date on Robert's declining health and the exploits of their children. Once peace was agreed, Fanny hoped to travel to the South of France for the sake of Robert's health and would visit Katy en route. Now *that* she looked forward to.

Cathy was made aware of another name from the past. She heard that Elisabeth Vigée Le Brun had returned to Paris for the first time since her hurried departure twelve years previously. She had even managed to return to her hôtel Le Brun despite her divorced husband having claimed it. Cathy resolved to visit her and found the interior restored to the tasteful glamour that she had always associated with the painter. Elisabeth had spent the years in the great capitals of Europe, most recently in St Petersburg, painting the aristocracy, no doubt for lavish sums. The visit was a mistake. Elisabeth was polite if somewhat distant and kept strewing aristocratic names around like rose petals. She assumed Cathy shared her poor opinion of the Paris fashions and Cathy was left with the impression that the famous Vigée Le Brun was trapped in time, as reflected in her portraits. It was a pity. She hesitated to mention young Lawrence's work that she had seen in London, and Elisabeth admitted she had yet to visit London and was glad that peace would give her the opportunity. Cathy left without any wish to further renew the acquaintance.

'Louis Otto tells me that there are some 70,000 French prisoners in England due to be returned to France,' mentioned Charles one day. 'I had no idea there were so many. Mainly sailors held in the hulks of rotting ships. Apparently they are in a very sorry state. He asks if we can prevail on Bonaparte to have them treated as well as his invalid veterans.' It prompted Catherine to ask how the prisoners in France were treated.

'I have no idea,' which was a rare remark from Charles. 'I'll look into it.'

He was pleased with himself when he reported back to her the following week that he had agreed with Bonaparte that the Russian prisoners should be well fed and equipped with new uniforms before being repatriated. 'That should impress the new Tsar Alexander!' Diplomacy took many forms.

—⁂—

It was Joseph Bonaparte who signed the British peace treaty with Lord Cornwallis at Amiens. When the document arrived in Paris, Talleyrand enjoyed teasing Napoleon by not producing it until the conclusion of the Council's business that morning. It was a display of confidence in his relationship with the First Consul that astounded others, not least Cathy. From then on emissaries from all over Europe paid court to Talleyrand and Cathy basked in his reflected glory. Of the English touring aristocracy, Cathy was delighted to meet Lady Bessborough, whose own affairs made her such a broad-minded guest, and Beth Armitage, Charles Fox's mistress, whom he only now admitted he had recently married for the purpose of the visit. Beth knew the social handicap of being a mistress to an eminent politician and being childless as his wife. So Cathy was particularly pleased to entertain her while Mr Fox rummaged the French archives for his biography of James II.

The only sour note was struck when Charles confessed to her that Bonaparte had passed on to him the complaints of certain dignitaries about having to be received by the Foreign Minister's mistress. Bonaparte had been voted First Consul for life and 'Napoleon', as he now styled himself, monarch-like, wanted his court to be more 'correct' than any other in Europe. Charles admitted Napoleon had told him that it was time he either married Mme Grand or dropped her. It alarmed Cathy. She knew that was more a command than advice. Charles knew it too and moved to reopen his case with Pius VII. He wrote expressing some penitence and quoting precedence for married bishops that he had diligently researched. Cathy was unsure which had cost him the most effort.

In the meantime she visited Joséphine Bonaparte, outlining their intent to legally marry and asking her to plead patience with her husband on their behalf. Joséphine was more than happy to act as the intermediary for the lovers. They waited anxiously for a reply from Rome. It still had yet to arrive when an unexpected visitor from England was announced: Mr George Grand. It was like a voice from the dead for Cathy. Charles was all for sparing her the interview, but Cathy wanted to be part of it.

'Hello, Katy, you're looking well.'

'Thank you, George.'

She could hardly reciprocate. He looked a lot older; he had put on weight and the Indian climate had not treated his complexion kindly. George looked around the anteroom into which he had been shown. Cathy was aware that the elegance of the hôtel Gallifet matched the splendour of any princely Indian palace he would know. As he talked, she was reminded of his mannerisms and his accented French. He was politeness itself. So much so that Cathy wondered whether there was a point to this visit. Charles shuffled in his chair and intervened to ask what brought him to Paris. His reasons were soon apparent and as mercenary as Cathy had remembered of him. Charles was able to bring the meeting to a mercifully short conclusion, promising George that he would see what he could do for him. Charles would have a proposal with him at his hôtel du Cercle in rue de Richelieu soon. Once he had been escorted to the door, Cathy joined Charles in a much-needed cognac.

Charles had evidently anticipated this eventuality and told Cathy his plan. 'Despite the State divorce, he could still be an embarrassment to us. However, he is clearly amenable to being bought off. What I have in mind is a suitable sinecure as far away as possible. He has been overseas long enough not to view that as exile, but rather as retirement. At least that is how I shall propose it.'

'Can you do that? I do not owe George anything but I would like him to be at least comfortable.'

'I could prevail on our Dutch associates to give him some titular post back in one of their colonies.'

Not surprisingly, given the subjugate status of the Bavarian Republic, the Dutch were prepared to offer Mr Grand the post of special consultant to Cape Town on a salary of 2,000 florins, though the British were still in the process of vacating it under the terms of the treaty. The offer was accepted and Mr Grand made his way to Amsterdam. If the newspapers were aware of his visit, they knew better than to mention it.

—◦—

That July, the papal reply finally reached Charles at the spa town and he shared the contents with Cathy. It advised him that the Curia found that none of the precedents that Talleyrand had quoted bore any real analogy to his case. While it permitted

'Citizen Maurice Talleyrand, Minister of Foreign Relations, to be returned to secular and laical life', it went on to confirm that no bishop had ever received a dispensation to marry.

'What does that mean?'

Charles was thoughtful. He said it had been carefully worded so as to ensure no other bishop should ever seek to use his marriage as a precedent. On the other hand he believed that, by giving him absolution and allowing him to cast aside his bishop's vows, he could get married in his confirmed secular state. It was not as definite as they would have liked but Napoleon was delighted to hear it.

Cathy agreed with Charles that it was to be a private wedding with a few suitable guests. The marriage contract was drawn up at Neuilly bestowing a sizeable dowry on Cathy, and was witnessed by the First Consul and Joséphine, as well as the two other consuls and Talleyrand's two younger brothers. The following day, on 10th September 1802, at the arrondissement's Town Hall, Charles Maurice de Talleyrand-Perigord, aged forty-eight, married Catherine-Noel Worlée, aged thirty-nine, divorced wife of George Francis Grand, as duly reported by *Le Journal des Hommes Libres*.

What was not published was that the day after that civic marriage, Charles and Cathy made their way to the church of St Médard's in Epinay-sur-Seine. It was as dilapidated a church as any in Paris after so many years of neglect and, being a Saturday, there were no worshippers present. Charles had arranged it with the curé, Abbé Pourez, and they were duly married by him, as witnessed by both Charles's friend Radix Sainte-Foy and the Prince of Nassau-Siegen who happened to be in Paris seeking a new naval command. Doubtless Abbé Pourez was handsomely rewarded for his silence. Whatever the opinions, whether jealous or scandalised, of others, Cathy and Charles were absolutely delighted to be officially man and wife.

When Cathy was later introduced at court as Mme de Talleyrand, Napoleon, never known for his tact with regard to women, said he 'hoped the dignified conduct of Mme de Talleyrand would soon replace the frivolity of Mme Grand'. To which Charles replied that, indeed, 'she could do no better than follow the example of Mme Bonaparte'. Cathy had arrived at last.

Valençay

Cathy was reclining on her new Egyptian-style chaise longue, absently stroking her pug, 'Pitt', as Charles joined her. 'You look reflective. What are you thinking about?' he asked. She lay the dog down, smoothed her dress and sat up.

'I was thinking of the time when we were in England and how much has changed in the past ten years. We were outcasts then and now…' she left the sentence unfinished. He sat down beside her.

'And now, Mme Talleyrand, the carriages of half the aristocracy of Europe jostle to enter our gates,' he said with a gesture to the courtyard below.

'Does that not make you happy?' she asked.

'Happy?' He looked out of the window. 'I think the happiest days of my life were in the years leading up to the fall of the Bastille. Life has become complicated since.'

She had to ask, 'Do I not make you happy?'

'Of course, my dear! But I cannot be with you all the time.' Ever the diplomat, she thought, but he gave her happiness and she too would have to look back to that pre-Revolutionary period to feel as carefree and cared for.

As Mme de Talleyrand, Cathy hosted any number of soirées and petit-soupers at their Neuilly villa for not only diplomats but any visitors distinguished by their station or talents. From the comments reported back to her, she knew such gatherings were viewed as among the most select in France, on a par with those of Consuless Joséphine or the salon of Juliette Récamier. However gauche Cathy had been, or seemed to have been, under the Directory, she now had a reputation for tact and conventional propriety that went down well with those guests whose own backgrounds expected such in others. Napoleon had made it clear that he expected respectability in his officials and that meant their women should know their place. It was a constraint most of them were not used to.

Not surprisingly, then, news of a novel that took up their cause spread rapidly. It was *Delphine* by Mme de Staël. Cathy asked Charles about it. 'Germaine de Staël had written many books, all fulminating against whichever faction was in power at the time,' Charles said dismissively.

'But this is not about politics.' Charles confessed he had read it and that it may not purport to be about politics but was certainly an attack on the current administration's policies.

'So, you have read it?' she asked.

'Oh yes. I recognised that the woman "Mme de Vernon" is a caricature of myself,' he affirmed reluctantly. Like the caricatures sold by Mr Holland, Cathy recalled, with all the worst aspects exaggerated. She borrowed his copy, read it through carefully and recognised that the heroine's most intimate friend, Mme de Vernon, concealed ruthless greed and egoism under a mask of vapid charm and sensibility. While Cathy thought it grossly unfair, she was gratified to note her former rival could never be reconciled to Charles after this. But there was more to this book than that and she tackled Charles again:

'Did you read how a woman wants happiness, but a man prefers reputation. His love is never unqualified? That is what we were talking about the other day.' Charles did not disagree. Rather, he took the view that Mme de Staël saw that as making women superior, that their romanticism was key to the best liberal politics. Cathy feared she might be getting out of her depth but persisted. 'I did not see her view of women as being superior or inferior. Rather, I saw it as a cry for the right of women to be themselves and not judged by a different code than from men. It was you who gave me Wollstonecraft's book, you remember.'

Charles smiled at the memory. 'So I did! Still, we may well get to that utopian form of society eventually. But, for now, we are where we are.'

Where they were was not uncomfortable. Cathy did not feel she was treated as an inferior by Charles. She felt much more self-assured now that they were married, secure and respected. She thought they could look forward to the future with more confidence. When they were together at Sains-du-Nord, her Piédcourt was every bit the loving husband, but even at the annual break at Bourbon l'Archembault, he could become the grand seigneur, minister to the First-Consul-for-Life. There was peace, certainly, but Charles seemed busier than ever. While Napoleon believed peace could be assured by constant pressure on Britain and Austria, Charles was more of the opinion that conciliation and moderation were greater guarantees that it would last. He was forever placating the British ambassador, Lord Whitworth, every time he complained about some deemed provocation. Personally, Cathy dreaded having to meet the British ambassador's wife who barely disguised her dislike of having to be polite to her. Lady Arabella Whitworth had that inbred prejudice that Eleanor, and even Fanny, had warned her to expect of the old moneyed aristocracy of England.

Fortunately, other visitors were much more welcome and none more so than the Craufords. Quintin and Eleanor duly arrived in Paris together with four of Quintin's nephews about whom Cathy had heard so much. Sir James Crauford was not among the party; Eleanor had explained that he was in the process of handing over to his successor in Hamburg. Quintin Crauford was duly charmed by Talleyrand who was delighted to meet a Briton of wide interests and with a similar belief in the value of a peaceful and stable France. Of course there were differences of opinion on how that should be, and they enjoyed discussing European politics well into the evening, over a quality wine that had long been absent in England. Eleanor, in the meantime, wanted to know all about Cathy and Charles: 'To think that it all started in Kensington Square! I would never have guessed it.' They talked about Paris and how different it was from pre-Revolutionary days. And Neuilly. Eleanor was not at all jealous. She took some pride in having helped Cathy along her journey to this fulfilment of her dreams. For her part, Cathy was pleased to have a friend she could confide in so readily. If that had started in rue du Sentier, Cathy too would never have guessed it. All too soon it was time to part. Charles wished there were more Englishmen like Quintin. He could do business with the likes of him. 'That's because he is Scottish!' Cathy retorted with a laugh.

There were any number of official visits to hôtel Gallifet by dignitaries from the four corners of Europe and Cathy could not help but admire how Charles managed to cope with the strain of adopting a different manner according to the country representative he was dealing with. He had explained to her that there was a need to properly organise the new Batavian, Helvetic and Cisalpine republics so that they could be stable states, which could easily be misinterpreted by the major monarchies or emperors as a wish to undermine their own establishments. On the other hand, he could feel justifiably aggrieved that Britain had called a halt to vacating Cape Town, Pondicherry and Malta as required by the treaty. As mutual mistrust grew, he was ever trying to sooth the ruffled feathers of the relevant ambassador on the one hand and the First Consul on the other. It was a relief when Napoleon despatched him to effect the reorganisation of the several hundred German fiefdoms on the right bank of the Rhine in compensation for the French annexation of those on the left bank. Cathy was not surprised at how much he welcomed the commission in every sense.

'But you do not speak German,' she cautioned.

'No, but, believe me, they are rushing to learn French!' he assured her.

It was while she was on her own in Paris that she received an invitation to visit Consuless Joséphine at her Malmaison chateau. Cathy was suitably impressed by the splendour of the estate but more so by the informality of her reception. From her few visits to the Tuileries, she had expected the same pomp and etiquette that reinforced the grandeur of the First Consul. But this was Joséphine's domain, a relaxing tribute to her interest in botany and harmony. It was a pleasure to talk to Joséphine without having to worry about any possible misinterpretation of word or action. The only awkward dialogue was when the question of succession was referred to. Cathy knew Joséphine had her own children, but it was clear the lack of any from Napoleon was a real concern. Cathy was relieved that Charles was not concerned for an heir, or did not seem to be. This beautiful estate was some compensation for the Consuless though, and Cathy learnt that it was a different Napoleon when he was here. He was a cheerful and amiable companion with a genial delight in what was being cultivated. Cathy took note and could not help but express the wish that Charles could be more relaxed away from the affairs of state too.

Charles's letters to her had included mention of the growing success of his German negotiations, which resulted in over 200 independent cities, states or bishoprics being consolidated into forty geographically simpler territories. It was a massive transfer of ownership, which would simplify the multi-coloured jumble of countries that Tom had first pointed out to her when introducing her to the map of Europe. Charles looked tired on his return to Paris; though behind that casual façade he was absolutely jubilant. The consolidation of so many principalities had netted him a tidy sum as well as reducing the Austrian Empire's hold on Germany. It was gratifying to have his efforts duly confirmed by what was still referred to as the Holy Roman Empire at the end of February.

Prior to that, Napoleon had already become frustrated with Spain over its prevarication in transferring Louisiana back to France. He had been approached by President Jefferson's representatives keen to improve relations ahead of the transfer. It prompted Napoleon to reconsider his plans for France's colony in the New World, the safety of which could not be easily guaranteed in the event of further war. Well aware of his Foreign Minister's views on colonies rather than conquests, and also how easily upset the Americans had been last time they were faced with his commission request, Napoleon deliberately kept Talleyrand out of the negotiations. Whatever the sale price, there was the added benefit that it could secure

America as an ally should the need arise. Talleyrand could not agree and made his lone opposition clear. Cathy thought it a sign of how secure they were that he could do so. Few others would dare.

But it was a jubilant Charles who greeted her a few days later. 'Cathy, my dear, we are to have a palace, a huge country estate of our own!' He explained, 'Napoleon has insisted that I take over chateau de Valençay, an estate south of the Loire valley, but somewhere more suitable than Neuilly for us to host the more important foreign aristocracy.'

'But what is wrong with Neuilly?'

'This is a whole different magnitude. It has fully a hundred rooms and vast hectares. There will be any number of staff to organise. Doubtless there will redecoration and repairs to effect. It will be at last a domain worthy of the Talleyrand-Perigords!'

Cathy was pleased for him, of course, but uncertain of its necessity. 'Can we afford it?'

'No, even if I sell the Neuilly villa. However, Napoleon has offered to give me the balance, which is substantially all. It is an offer I can hardly refuse.' It sounded too good to be true and Cathy did wonder whether her conversation with Joséphine had prompted it.

'I still do not understand why he should be so generous,' said Cathy. Charles felt piqued that she should so undervalue his worth. Had he not completely reshaped Germany and thus constrained Austria? Perhaps it was a bribe by Napoleon to ensure the ongoing support of his Foreign Minister, similar to the Louisiana sale, thought Cathy, ever mindful of the growing European tensions.

—⁂—

Sure enough, that May, matters came to a head with Britain. Charles knew that England had been busy making overtures to Russia and Austria to consider a third coalition against France and had done his best to convince Lord Whitworth of Napoleon's peaceful intentions. However, Whitworth was aware of his own government's intentions and asked for his passport, the usual preliminary to a declaration of war. Charles pleaded with him but to no avail. Napoleon was presented with an ultimatum to withdraw from the Netherlands, and the expected refusal to do so resulted in Britain declaring war on France, after only fourteen months or so of peace. Charles was philosophical. 'It was probably inevitable but I, and indeed Napoleon, hoped we could have peace for a lot longer than it has lasted. It is now for me to ensure Prussia remains neutral.'

Only then, when Englishmen still in France faced internment, did Cathy receive a letter from Fanny Chambers explaining that Robert had died and she was alone in the South of France. Could she come and see her in Paris? When Fanny arrived, Cathy greeted her like the long-lost friend that she was.

'Well, Fanny, your French has improved!' She got an emotional reaction.

'Katy, it is so good to see you, though I never dreamed it would be in such circumstances. We thought Robert's health would improve in the Midi. But it was no use. He died only last week and I am stranded here and the route home closed by the war.'

She went into further detail and Cathy comforted her. Cathy was flattered that Fanny felt she could turn to her. She was not only pleased to see her old friend, but delighted to have the opportunity to give something back for the support she had received from Fanny when at her lowest ebb in Chandernagore.

It should be easy for her to procure the necessary passport and she could even provide a coach to the coast. Better still, she could accompany her, stopping en route at Sains-du-Nord. It would be a real pleasure. She had heard a fishing boat from a Dutch port was least likely to be impounded by the British, especially in the herring season, and proposed that Fanny take that route.

Fanny looked around at the splendour of her surroundings. The décor was an extravagant, if not gaudy, mixture of neo-classical and ancien régime.

'Are you happy, Katy?'

Cathy was surprised by the question. Of course she should be happy. She had to think about it.

'Oh, Katy, I'm sorry. It is impertinent of me. It's just that I do not see this' – and she gestured at the furniture and furnishings – 'as being you. I remember you as you were in Calcutta.'

'Have I changed so much?'

'I'm sure we both have. It would be hard not to. Returning to England was a shock for me. We are treated as "nabobs", over-rich outsiders, by a small-minded society which has no idea of the responsibility Robert had to take and what he accomplished for Bengal justice. It weighed him down and I believe is the reason for his premature death.'

'I'm so sorry, Fanny.' Cathy wanted to share her 'homecoming' reactions. 'I know what you mean by being treated as an outsider by jealous gossips, especially, in my case, when I was merely a "mistress from the Indies" to a powerful diplomat. Still, I like to think that success has not gone to my head. Though I sometimes wonder about Charles.' She was thinking of Valençay. Fanny could sense the conversation was getting too personal and changed the subject. They discussed Cathy's arrangements for Fanny to return to England and in no time at all Cathy had organised it.

The Talleyrand coach took them in comfort to Sains-du-Nord. From there they took a post-chaise through to the Batavian Republic with 'Pitt' the pug to discourage idle curiosity. Although few spoke French north of Brussels, Fanny was surprised to find English more commonly understood once they crossed the river Waal. Casual enquiries about the effectiveness of the English blockade led them to go further north to the fishing town of Katwijk-aan-Zee. Here, Fanny found a fisherman who might, for a price, be willing to take her on his fishing *buss*, as the boat was called, with a view to landing his catch, with Fanny, at Lowestoft. Cathy's offer of indemnity, should his boat be impounded by the Royal Navy, clinched the deal. The last embrace of the ladies was a long one. Fanny wiped a tear from her eye. 'You have been a true friend. I cannot thank you enough. It is dreadful to think we may not meet again.'

'Nonsense! You remember you said the same thing in Calcutta.' The two forty-something-year-olds parted with the same affection as they had shared in their teens.

Once again, as Cathy returned from the Batavian Republic, she had to circumvent the army moving north-east, though now at least there appeared to be less urgency and her post-chaise was generally given enough room to pass. Once again, Charles was relieved to have her safely back in Paris. He explained that it had been decided to occupy King George's Hanover dominion, though Hamburg itself, being an independent Hanseatic city, would not be included. That was reassuring to both of them. If anything, it made it easier to visit Herr Warburg.

As Britain was alone in going to war with France, the continent remained peaceful through that winter. Napoleon had marshalled an ever-increasing army along the Channel coast with every show of preparing for an invasion while the Royal

Navy demonstrated its control of the seas, not least in the West Indies. Its blockade of the key ports around the continent made little difference to the civilian population. Certainly there was no shortage of the necessities of life in Paris. As Charles said, they now had time to visit their new Valençay property. It set Cathy wondering how she would run such a massive establishment as well as her existing responsibilities. She would need a first class and trustworthy bailiff of some sort. Charles assured her she need not worry and, as their coach left the Loire Valley at Orléans, she began to pay more attention to the unfolding countryside. They crossed the Cher at Selles-sur-Cher and were soon on their own estate. Not surprisingly, they were given a gracious welcome there as the staff and tenant farmers looked to please their new landlord and his fetching wife.

Charles left Cathy to it and returned to Paris where he became increasingly wrapped up in making himself indispensable to Napoleon, more so than Joseph Fouché, if possible. There was always an occasional plot against Napoleon; that was to be expected. So Cathy was as surprised as others to be told that General Moreau had been arrested as complicit in the latest plot. Charles said a Bourbon prince was also implicated. It was a shock to her when it became apparent that Charles had been the instigator of his kidnap from across the border resulting in his summary execution in Paris. It brought back memories of the previous revolutionary regimes and she was not convinced by Charles's justifications to her. As Foreign Minister, Charles was aware that it had shocked the rest of Europe too and that Napoleon's carefully nurtured image as the founder of a new, enlightened Roman-style Republic was seriously marred. Indeed, public opinion was such that General Moreau was acquitted. The more Charles made light of the prince's execution as a totally just end to a plot on Napoleon, the more Cathy worried. This was not the same Talleyrand that had praised the moderation of General Bonaparte.

In the absence of any conflict to speak of, preparations got under way to establish Napoleon as the head of a new French dynasty, only eleven years after decapitating the last hereditary monarch. Clearly the title 'King' would not do, especially for the head of what was still nominally a republic. On the other hand, France now had the territorial reach of an Austrian or Ottoman Empire. It was only fitting that Caesar should become Augustus, an emperor. Once again a referendum demonstrated the French support for this, without needing the usual creative inflation of the votes. Various new imperial titles were distributed and Charles was proud to tell Cathy he was to be the empire's first Grand Chamberlain. She congratulated him, reflecting it really was impressive how, despite his obvious handicap, he had managed to adapt to different regimes, literally keep his head, and come out on top. If changing to suit the latest administration meant being less honest with oneself, she understood. As a woman in a decidedly man's world, she appreciated how much one had to sacrifice a bit of dignity to survive whenever adversity strikes. For Cathy, the only important facet of her Piédcourt was his affection for, and loyalty to, her.

Her calm was interrupted that October when she found Charles unusually furious over some incident. 'They've kidnapped Sir George Rumbold and he's being held in The Temple. How could they!' Cathy thought that a bit rich coming from the instigator of the kidnap of that Bourbon prince only seven months earlier.

'Is he going to be executed?'

'*Mon Dieu, non*! Not if I can help it!' he said vehemently.

'No?' asked Cathy in mock surprise. Charles chose to ignore the implied reference to his previous involvement with a previous political abduction.

'So, who is Sir George Rumbold?' she asked.

'He is the British ambassador to Hamburg. They believe Hamburg to be the centre of British plotting on the continent.'

Suddenly, Cathy was alarmed. 'But what makes them think that?'

'I have no idea. It's Fouché's operation and he is normally well informed.'

'But surely Hamburg is independent. He has no right.'

Charles explained how the French soldiers had crossed the Elbe, broken into Rumbold's house (I know it well, thought Cathy) and brought him and his files forcibly here to Paris. 'Hamburg may be a free city but Prussia, as guardian of the free cities, will be furious and I can expect its ambassador, Marquis Lucchesini – you know, the same who was our guest at Valençay only last month – to vent his fury on me shortly. It could undo all the work I have put in to keep Prussia out of the war.'

Cathy was less concerned about Lucchesini than how much Rumbold's files might disclose what she did for his predecessor, Sir James Crauford. If her Piédcourt had some idea as to her involvement, then he had never raised the matter. It was important that, as the recently promoted Grand Chamberlain of the Empire, he be protected from the same sort of accusation that had landed her in prison six years previously. Cathy feigned a calm that she did not feel.

'What will you do? You must get him released. I know too well how much he must hate being in that prison. He must be fearing the worst!'

Charles moved uncharacteristically fast to resolve the situation. The following morning he obtained Napoleon's authority to have Rumbold released from The Temple and despatched to Cherbourg where a cutter under a flag of truce would transfer him to one of the blockading British frigates.

'But that will take days,' she said. 'Surely Le Havre or Calais would be quicker.'

'True. But this way he cannot fail to notice the strength of our army all along the coast. It is Napoleon's idea.'

She had to ask, 'What about his files?'

'Fouché has them. That, after all, was the point of the expedition.'

It worried her. She struggled to keep composed and concentrate on her daily routine. Eventually, some days later when Charles was more relaxed, she ventured to ask him, 'Was there any substance to the story about the British using Hamburg as a base for spying?' He gave her his knowing smile.

'We knew it was, of course. That bundle of documents proves it, though most of the plotters were arrested at the time of the Moreau conspiracy. Hence the embarrassment of the British government, which they covered up by making such a big fuss over our handling of it. The documents also include the granting of passports to England for our spies pretending to offer their services to the British, including one of mine that Fouché was unaware of. Rest assured, he will be more interested in that than if there is any passing reference to your visits to Herr Moses.' He winked at her.

What a web of deception, thought Cathy. I was a relatively innocent bystander, not even a pawn in that game. 'That is a relief,' she agreed and was happy to return to the pleasurable chores of the wife of the Grand Chamberlain.

Her Piédcourt was enjoying himself even if it meant being tied to rue du Bac. Cathy had got used to spending weeks, if not months, on their Valençay estate managing the army of retainers as the chateau and grounds were restored to their former glory. While she was mindful that its purpose was to further flatter foreign dignitaries, Cathy also felt it should be their country home and reflect their own aristocratic sensibilities, be they Perigord or Worlée. She was particularly pleased to have established a school for girls. It was all very well for the likes of Wollstonecraft and de Staël to write about the importance of women; she would actually do something about it.

Gradually she got to know the tenant farmers and the craftsmen. She so appreciated these breaks from holding receptions that she would happily change into riding breeches and tour a section of the 12,000 hectares as a deliberate alternative to the strain of acting the gracious hostess of the Grand Chamberlain. She had made a point of telling the Empress Joséphine how much Valençay meant to her. She understood more than anyone. Cathy remembered that Fanny had asked her whether she was happy. Here in Valençay, the answer would always be 'Yes'.

Benevento

Cathy looked at herself critically in the mirror. It was no use pretending she had the same gorgeous looks at forty-one that she had had at thirty-one. Good living had left its mark, however carefully she tried. And she had tried. She spent a lot of trouble over her make-up and such stylish clothes that made the best of her figure. We have mellowed together, thought Cathy. Charles still paid her the same attention but Cathy sensed there were other things on his mind that made him more dutiful as a husband than adoring. Perhaps it was her, though. She would make more of an effort to be the devoted wife and a proud consort to the Grand Chamberlain. They definitely still got on. When it came to planning Napoleon's coronation as Emperor, she showed as much enthusiasm as she could. Apparently, the Pope had been invited to perform the actual crowning in a way that would be a deliberate echo of Charlemagne's acceptance of the crown from the then Pope all those centuries ago. Cathy was not keen to meet this obstacle to her marriage. She heard that he shared her reluctance.

She could not be but secretly amused when, at almost the last minute, the Pope insisted that Napoleon should marry

Joséphine in a church ceremony before they would be crowned. After all, Joséphine had been Bonaparte's civic wife longer than Cathy had been Talleyrand's partner. But she was pleased for them and genuinely happy to be part of the deliberately awe-inspiring coronation ceremony that December. It snowed over Paris that morning but no one minded. The long procession consisted of the great from every establishment as well as, naturally, the army in their splendid and varied uniforms. There were enough official guests crowded into the recently repaired Notre Dame Cathedral to replace the winter chill with a convivial warmth and there were fireworks and festivities to follow. It was in the early hours of the following morning that the Talleyrands returned to rue du Bac. Charles sank into his favourite chair.

'I'm getting too old for these late nights!'

'Me too, but it was worth it. What an occasion! And the Emperor only thirty-five. I liked the way he crowned Joséphine Empress. Didn't she look stunning?'

Charles reached for her hand. 'As did you, my dear.' He massaged his lame leg. 'Napoleon certainly deserves it. He has achieved so much these last, what, five years?'

'So have you, Charles.'

Charles nodded. 'So has everyone there at the cathedral today,' he said. 'Every one of them self-made men, mostly from humble families. None there by birth.' And their self-made ladies, thought Cathy, with equal pride.

—✲—

It seemed like no time before it was spring and the streets of Paris basked in the brighter days. Never had Charles spent so much time with Napoleon. What they discussed, Cathy never knew, nor cared. The war seemed unreal to her, consisting, as it did, largely of a blockade of the French ports by the Royal Navy while Pitt tried to rebuild a coalition with promises of subsidies. Charles showed her the caricature that Napoleon had commissioned of an Englishman offering money to anyone who would take it. When Cathy said how she had first come across such caricatures in London, and was surprised at their popularity, Charles admitted there was an English caricature of the coronation which featured both of them in the forefront of the procession. Cathy was intrigued, but Charles said he had not kept the copy shown to him and, besides, it grossly exaggerated his short foot. Cathy wanted to know more.

'What of me does it exaggerate?' she asked.

'Oh, it had you all wrong. The caption described you as the former Mrs Halhed.'

'Halhed? Who's he?'

Charles had no idea who he was, and Cathy realised it was as well that whoever had commissioned the caricature had no idea of her background. Still, it was amusing to think she was significant enough to be featured in the window of Mr Holland's shop in London, however unflattering.

Their Valençay estate was taking up more of her time and Charles was delighted for her, not least when she reported the sort of income it could generate. Their concerns about being able to afford it were replaced by a glow of pride in ensuring it could be restored to self-sufficiency. Cathy had made it her project and, after a few faltering faux-pas, found she could handle all the many issues of running such a diverse enterprise, including vineyards and cheese production, with the respect of both its field and chateau staff. Charles was content to let her manage it while he concentrated on the Emperor and his affairs. Thus it was no surprise to her that Charles accompanied Napoleon on his journey to Lombardy to receive the crown of Italy that May. He returned a few weeks later.

'Rumour has it that you had an affair with Mme Simons while in Milan,' Cathy was cautiously amused as they relaxed in the warm July sunshine at Bourbon-l'Archamboult.

'Poor little Elise! She's like a girl in a musical chairs game who suddenly found herself without a chair when the music stopped,' Charles replied. 'I'm told that rumour also had it I died there. But as you can see that is not true either!' He smiled. 'Besides, Napoleon kept me far too busy. We even visited Marengo, though there's little to remind one of the battle there five years ago. He told me how he had almost lost that one.'

'What would have happened if he had, I wonder?' mused Cathy.

'The fragile Consulate would have collapsed and us with it. Then the Bourbon monarchy would have been re-introduced with all its feudal paraphernalia. Thank God he won.' Charles said decidedly.

He was in a pensive mood. 'One thing I have learnt in my tours is that, however much Napoleon is cheered as a victor, his real attribute is as a law giver. It is because he has brought them a sensible legal Code that ordinary people can live and trade with more confidence than they did before. I've always thought Peace is enough, but it's Justice that keeps it.' Cathy reflected on that.

'I know what you mean. It is what Fanny said her Robert accomplished best for Bengal.' It reminded her. 'Do you think we shall ever recover our settlements in India?'

'I doubt it. They are as difficult to defend as Louisiana. Napoleon's eastern ambition disappeared when he evacuated

Egypt.' Cathy wondered about her sister and her family. She very much doubted they would meet again.

They returned to Paris and the usual round of entertaining and being entertained. The army, '*La Grande Armée*' as it was being referred to, was still camped all along the coast, though Charles assured Cathy that the likelihood of it ever invading England was always in doubt as long as the Royal Navy remained in control of the seas. It was not a complete stalemate, he cautioned, as he had heard Lord Harrowby was actively encouraging, bribing Charles called it, the emperors of Russia and Austria to join in what would be a third coalition. Since Charles had masterminded treaties with Baden, Württemberg and Bavaria for Napoleon, he had a particular interest in countering Harrowby's advances to the King of Prussia. Fortunately Lucchesini, a friend as much as the Prussian ambassador, shared Charles's fervent wish that a continental clash be avoided. It may not be enough. Napoleon instructed Charles to offer Hanover to the King of Prussia with a time limit to the offer. It must have been tempting to the Prussian king; but perhaps offending King George was too great a risk. The offer lapsed but Prussia did affirm its neutrality. Charles was content with that. More remarkably, the king of Naples also pledged his neutrality though, as Charles explained to Cathy, he had not stopped an Anglo-Russian force then occupying Naples. She noted how Charles remained unperturbed by the escalating hostilities, and guessed, hoped even, that he mirrored his master's confidence.

Once again Russia and Austria set about ponderously assembling vast armies and equipment under fifty-three-year-old Mack and sixty-year-old Kutusov. The storm finally broke at the end of August as the Austrian army invaded Bavaria. 'Here we go again,' Charles told Cathy. Sure enough, the well-trained, if bored, French army on the coast under Corps commanders whose average age was thirty-nine, left the Channel and crossed France to take up positions on the Rhine. Napoleon, still a young thirty-six-year-old, then left Paris with Joséphine and Talleyrand included in his entourage, catching up with his army on 1ˢᵗ October.

Charles's first letter to Cathy told her how Napoleon had left them both behind at Strasbourg saying how 'distressing it was to leave the two persons we love best'. It was clear from his subsequent letters that her Charles was more impressed by, and fearful for, Napoleon than had been evident for some time. Cathy shared his concern but for a different reason. Back in Paris rumours that the Bank of France had run out of reserves had prompted fears that its money was going to be as valueless as the Republic's assignats. Another Marengo was needed to restore confidence.

It was not long in coming. Within a couple of weeks the Grande Armée had surrounded the Austrian army at Ulm on the Danube and forced its surrender. Charles, still in Strasbourg, passed on the news to Cathy and told her how he had immediately written to Napoleon with his plan for a peace. She knew he would have urged restraint and some territorial reallocation in order to best avoid a renewal of war. It seemed Charles already had heard the disappointing news from Cadiz of the British navy's victory at Trafalgar. He told Cathy he was leaving for Munich, recently occupied by Bernadotte, in order to talk to Napoleon face to face. Through his letters, Cathy learned of the particularly harsh October sleet and snow there, the scarcity of food and the dreadful condition of the roads. Eventually he caught up with the Emperor in Vienna, which had capitulated readily enough, and wrote to tell her he was hoping Napoleon would arrange an armistice so that they could discuss possible terms. That was followed by another letter, written hastily to contradict the earlier one: circumstances were against them. A combined Austro-Russian army was advancing from the east and represented a threat to what had so far been a flawless and almost bloodless campaign. A further blow to Charles's hopes was the news that the King of Prussia had just agreed to intervene on the side of Austria and Russia. Charles felt personally betrayed but all he could do was shiver in a cold Viennese November while the army moved north to Brno. She felt for him.

It was then that Cathy heard of Talleyrand's death. It was one of his younger brothers who brought her the news, which made it more credible. Cathy was distraught. This was not meant to happen. Her Piédcourt was a fifty-one-year-old civilian, unused to the rigours and deprivations of a winter campaign. When she had recovered sufficiently she considered carefully. It could again be a false rumour, as before. She resolved to visit the Empress Joséphine. She should have the latest news. It was speedily arranged.

The chateau de Malmaison looked very different in winter, though the orangery was heated well enough for her tropical fruits. It was there that the Empress received her. Cathy told her of the rumour about Charles and Joséphine was able to reassure her with what she knew. Certainly if Talleyrand had died, there would have been mention of it in Napoleon's more recent letters to her. There were always dreadful rumours about Napoleon too and she had come to dismiss them as the malicious title-tattle emanating from the royalists in the faubourg Saint-Germain. She invited Cathy to join a private gathering she held regularly for certain ladies whose husbands were serving in the Grande Armée.

It was the sort of informal dejeuner that Cathy had never experienced before. She knew a number of the ladies, many of them much younger than their hostess. There was Hortense, Jean Perregaux's daughter and the wife of General Marmont, and an even younger Louise Lannes. Charlotte Oudinot was more her own age. She recognised Aglaé Ney and her sister-in-law Marguerite from the time Charles had worked with Marshal Ney on the Mediation of the Helvetia Republic. There were others she did not recognise. Whatever their age and status, they had a common interest in wanting their husbands to survive this campaign. There was no frivolity here. News from recent letters was exchanged and any locations mentioned were identified on a map that Joséphine had arranged. On the one hand, Cathy, whose husband was unlikely to be within cannon shot of any engagement, felt an intruder. On the other, she felt privileged to be included in this female company for mutual support. She left much encouraged and more appreciative of Joséphine than she had expected.

Not long after, she received a letter from Charles confirming his uncomfortable existence in the Austrian capital. He made little mention of his attempts to offer advice to Napoleon but rather told her how he had managed to attend the premier of Beethoven's most recent work, *Fidelio*. The usual theatre patrons had mainly evacuated the city; so Charles had attended the opera in the company of some rowdy French and Bavarian officers. It had reminded him of Gaveaux's *Léonore* opera to which he taken Cathy to celebrate her release from prison. It was such good news to know that he was alive and, indeed, thinking of her. Cathy felt overcome with emotion and later returned to her routines in a happier frame of mind than she had experienced for weeks. The news of a great victory at Austerlitz made less impression on her, though she was as jubilant as the next Parisian that their army had defeated the combined armies of Austria and Russia. Oh, and that the value of stocks and currency had recovered. She was elated on both a personal and a general level.

Charles now shared with her the horrors of war he had witnessed. Phrases from his letter stuck in her mind, such as his description of Brno as 'a horrible place. There are four or five thousand wounded here. Great numbers of them die every day. Yesterday the stench was unbearable.' Charles was responsible for negotiating the peace at Pressburg on Napoleon's terms. It may not have been as conciliatory as Charles would have wished but, as he put it, the Austrians would sign anything now. It was duly signed after Christmas, only twenty-five days after the battle. It was clear that the third coalition against France was effectively ended. The British Prime Minister died the month after Austerlitz and for a while Cathy summoned her dog as 'chien-chien' rather than appear insensitive to Pitt's demise.

When Charles was eventually reunited with Cathy, she barely recognised him. Physically, though obviously tired, he looked much the same – he always had paid attention to how he looked – but it was with difficulty he could turn on the usual charm. Over the next few days, he let her know that he was more than unhappy with the destructive impact of the Emperor's restless genius. He was still shocked by what he had seen of warfare and its aftermath. That was one thing. But of more concern to him was Napoleon's disregard of his advice. He admired Napoleon for his undoubted talent still, but there was a new ruthlessness in his approach to diplomacy, which went against everything Charles had a reputation for.

'I know he has had enough of the Austrians breaking the treaties he has made with them each time and returning to the battlefield. They seem to have learnt nothing. This time he thinks a more drastic reduction of the Austrian Empire will drive the lesson home,' said Charles. 'But I cannot see the Emperor accepting the loss of so much Hapsburg land which they have owned for centuries. It sows the seed of another conflict.' Charles was particularly bitter about Prussia.

'They sided with the Austrians and Russians when they thought it advantageous and he rewards them with Hanover!' Clearly it was more important for Prussia to be alienated from Britain than to be punished for betraying the neutrality it had promised only four months previously.

Charles looked gloomy and Cathy ventured to ask whether he could do anything about it. 'We shall see,' was all he would answer and Cathy trusted that in his own way, and at his own pace, he would. For the moment though, the *Pax Gallica* had been extended and he returned to making foreign dignitaries recognise the value of it.

—⁂—

Cathy was glad to see that Charles soon regained his familiar civilised manner and how much he enjoyed being besieged by all the foreign ministers eager to pay homage to the most powerful member of Napoleon's cabinet. In particular, he learnt that the new British government included his friend, Charles Fox, as Foreign Secretary and that meant a chance to consider peace with England. In no time, they exchanged touching flattery of each other. Charles Talleyrand wrote how, France having no claims on English territory, a lasting peace was possible. Charles Fox replied that Talleyrand was the one man in Europe he would be happy to cooperate with. Talleyrand secured the release of

Englishmen detained since the start of war; Fox reported on a royalist plot to assassinate Napoleon. Cathy could see that, if he could secure peace, it would be her Piédcourt's crowning achievement. He confided in her the two main problems.

He had never felt Napoleon had been justified in handing over Hanover to Prussia, and the Emperor's view that it could be now offered to King George as a peace offering would create rather than solve a problem. Naturally, Prussia would not be keen to lose its new seaboard. Talleyrand's request that Prussia be included in the negotiation was rejected by the British Foreign Secretary. Nevertheless, Charles privately told Cathy he felt it was not an insurmountable issue. 'Prussia received Hanover out of fear and shall return it out of fear.' It seemed a bold assertion to Cathy.

The other issue was Fox's determination that Russia should be party to the negotiation, given Britain's treaty with the Tsar. Talleyrand agreed with his Emperor that this would be totally unacceptable. As Cathy was able to remind Charles, France had agreed that England could negotiate with France and her allies separately in 1782, so England should accept a similar separate negotiation in 1806. Inclusion of Russia in the negotiations was rejected by the French Foreign Minister. It was disappointing that the early prospect of a peace treaty should be so quickly foiled.

Her Piédcourt had lost none of his cunning, however. The Tsar had sent Baron Oubril to Paris to keep him informed of progress in the Franco-English discussions. Charles was delighted to welcome him, showered him with courteous flattery and within a few days had concluded a separate treaty with him as if the Tsar had given to Baron Oubril that authority. It opened the door for Fox to resume negotiations and the prospect of peace was once more tantalisingly close. The question of Hanover and appropriate compensation for Prussia remained, however, and would delay negotiations in the way that also brought back memories of 1782 to Cathy.

In the midst of these major concerns, Charles appeared one day to Cathy positively bursting with good humour. He had news of a more enjoyable nature. 'There are to be some fresh honours. The Marshals responsible for the victory already have the titles they were given when Napoleon became Emperor, so nothing new for them. Now, although Berthier is already a Marshal, he is to be Prince of Neufchatel and, you will love this, on condition he gets married, but not to his mistress the Marquise Visconti!'

'But that is so unfair,' stated Cathy predictably, 'after all —'

'Yes,' Charles interrupted, 'but you had an ally in high places, which she does not.'

'Well, I think they should go ahead regardless. Berthier is sufficiently in Napoleon's favour to force the issue!'

'We shall see. Anyway, the other aristocratic appointment is that Marshal Bernadotte, that scheming Jacobin, is bought off as Prince of Ponte-Corvo. Davout will be furious.' Charles was enjoying this. He got up and did a mock flourish.

'And now, let me introduce you to the future Prince de Benevento,' he said with a broad grin.

'Who?' she asked looking beyond him, as if she had not guessed by now.

'Why, me!'

'Oh and what or where is Benevento?'

He sat down again and explained. 'Napoleon thought it fitting that I should have the state of Benevento, which was a papal state before. It's his little joke because he knows I was reminding the Pope how I had restored that papal fiefdom to him at the time of the Concordat negotiations. Now it is to be mine. It's nothing really but it serves the Pope right for the trouble he gave me over the Concordat.'

'Oh, that *is* good; from bishop to owner of a papal principality! Or is it just an empty title?' asked Cathy.

'No, there is a dotation that goes with it. Not everyone gets the same. Napoleon has his favourites and, besides, some need it more than others. Benevento is good enough for us. Only some twenty to thirty thousand inhabitants,' he said waving his hand airily.

Cathy was staggered. '*Mon Dieu*, I should think so! How will we manage it? Do we have to move?'

'No, just visit when we can. I have in mind a governor for our principality, Louis de Beer. I'll introduce you once it becomes official.'

Cathy had a sudden thought. 'Does that make me a princess?'

'Of course!' He was amused by the pride she took in rehearsing the title. 'And what will their princess do for Benevento?' he asked lightly.

But Cathy took it seriously. 'I shall promote their goods, whatever they may be, and I shall found a school to educate its young ladies,' she said firmly.

Charles matched her mood. 'Well said. Educating women is one of the best ways to refine and uplift morals.'

Did he, the all-too-ready companion of bright young girls, mean it? Anyway, she did.

—⁂—

For the time being, however, there were the same affairs of State to be dealt with and the Prince of Benevento was still trying to salvage something of a fragile peace with Britain when news arrived of the death of Charles Fox. His British government colleagues had never shared his passionate interest in peace with Napoleon and the opportunity died with him. Cathy knew it was more of a disappointment to Charles than he cared to admit. At the same time Charles had to report to Napoleon that he heard Prussia was mobilising its military. Diplomatic business was never-ending and Cathy could only watch as her Piédcourt rode the crests and troughs with equal aplomb.

On one of the increasingly rare occasions they were together at Valençay, Cathy asked him, 'How do we rank among the nobility of Europe now?'

Charles took both her hands and raised them to his lips. He looked her in the eye. 'Order of precedence is not something to worry about, my dear. We French are different from the nobility of other monarchies and empires.'

She sensed something unusually heartfelt was being offered by her Piédcourt and stepped back. He steadied himself with his cane, and straightened up so as to appear more statesman-like, however domestic his surroundings. 'We take pride in knowing every imperial official achieved office by their talents, not their relatives.' He looked out of the window. 'Out there in the poorer *arrondissements* and further *départements* there are already the future princes, marshals, prefects, savants and,' he said, ending with his characteristic smile, 'even diplomats. That is what our Revolution has accomplished.'

'And princesses!' added the lady from Chandernagore.

Historical note

Apart from the memoires of George Grand and Tom Lewin, the evidence for Mme Grand is largely the vindictive comments made when she became attached to Talleyrand. Accordingly, biographers of the great man have been content to picture her as a dumb blond who seduced him and caused him only embarrassment, duly quoting the gossip. This is a pity as he *was* later seduced by a pretty young lady ('a man who marries his mistress creates a vacancy'), but she was the Duchess de Dino who ensured he separated from his wife and to whom he entrusted his memoires. That she heavily doctored them before releasing them for publication is a sad fact. It would also explain the absence of any positive mention of his wife.

Yet it is known that Talleyrand, ever ambitious, twice risked damaging his career on behalf of Catherine: once when she was imprisoned as a suspected spy; and again when he incurred Napoleon's wrath for causing a break in the negotiations for the Concordat by insisting on getting papal permission to marry Catherine. His biographers have chosen to view these as emotional aberrations in their intellectual hero, while recording his ready willingness to cast aside other ladies once he found them embarrassing. The only surviving mention of his love for any woman is the letter he wrote to Barras about Catherine which is duly included in Barras's memoires.

No one is sure when Catherine first met Talleyrand. I have taken his statement in London that he had met an English lady who could take his letters to avoid the Alien Office as enough of a clue that Mrs Grand was that lady.

There *was* a young out-of-work naval officer who recovered her Paris booty at the height of the Terror. It might test the credulity of the reader. So I have recast him as a freebooter who already had another motive to go to Paris. Just as gallant a feat, mind you.

Otherwise, the events and the persons mentioned are all real (even Ana the Portuguese maid). I have taken the liberty of giving them personas to fit the events. And I have had to make up for the gaps in her story. How did she and Tom get to Paris during the war? I have appointed him as secretary to the peace envoy. Nicolas de Lessart was the first Frenchman she was associated with when she eventually reached Paris. However, unknown to pre-internet historians, he *was* her family relative and not necessarily her lover. Who did she turn to in London? I have reintroduced Eleanora from her Paris days because of her Crauford connection.

Catherine is recorded as visiting Sir James Crauford in Hanover before and after Bonaparte's coup, but there is no evidence she engaged in underhand activity, though Olivier Blanc's *Les Espions de la Republique et de l'Empire* suggests so.

I am indebted to Casimir Carrère (*Talleyrand Amoureux*) for his research into the Talleyrands' secret church wedding. It demonstrates the former bishop's determination to be properly wedded to Catherine in the eyes of the Church as much as the State.

I have kept to the chronology of the period with the exception of the Frost Fair, which occurred the year after Talleyrand left for America. It would have been a shame for them to have missed it.